To my brothers.

Contents

Intro

What are your most valuable lessons? That's not an easy question to answer. The one I gave, however, resulted in this book you're about to read.

I'm not going to demand an answer from you, but I encourage you to start thinking. And I hope you can get some ideas as you move through these pages (perhaps you can share your answer once you're finished).

My own process of thinking began some years ago. Or, rather, I *experienced* something that later led me to the thinking-part. You see, the lessons I learned weren't obvious at first. I encountered them, but I didn't manage to articulate their meaning. It took some time before I fully understood what I had discovered. Now that I do, I want to share the story with you.

The lessons I learned are principles. That means that they're timeless modes of being that work irrespectively of historic time-periods, geographical locations, and even individual factors such as thoughts and feelings. They're undying in their nature, have worked for centuries, and will probably continue to work for centuries to come.

While I can't claim to know everything that is to know about these principles, I certainly know my own perspective.

The book follows the story of how I learned these lessons. It also describes their psychological underpinnings, as well as suggestions on how to apply them to your own life.

As I learned them from different perspectives, I felt it necessary to divide the books into parts. Part I includes the first three Notes; and is by far the darkest part of the book. It describes the birthing place of this journey, and how to heal from pain. Part II includes Note Four and Five and is a bit lighter than the previous section. It describes two valuable lessons on exposing oneself to a better life. Part III includes Note Six, Seven and Eight, and is a section that touches upon the freedom to live. Part IIII Includes the last Note. It describes how to achieve balance and it's the punctum of the journey.

Although there are many lessons to learn in a lifetime, there are at least nine I value at age 23. Let's explore them together.

Prologue

It was an early October morning. My schedule showed a lecture in 'statistics and quantitative research methods', but I decided to skip it due to the weather. It was beautiful.

Instead, I resolved to go for a walk. I put on my clothes and headed for the nearby forest. The sun was shining, and rays illuminated through the fog that hadn't cleared yet. As I walked, I rationalized this was a better use of my time than a dreary lecture in statistics.

As I moved along the forest trails, different thoughts came to my mind, and I began thinking of the book I was trying to write. I had been trying to write something for almost a year now, but I struggled. I couldn't settle on a concept, as there was too much I potentially wanted to write about.

Consequently, I never got far in the writing process either. I knew I wanted to write about something meaningful; something worthwhile and close to my heart, but I couldn't pinpoint what it was. It was making me frustrated (or perhaps I was just anxious about writing an entire book).

As I continued to walk through the forest, I further examined what I could write about to fill these criteria. Suddenly, however—I don't know how, but I guess my subconscious mind had been working hard to find a solution—an insight struck me. I thought, "What if I could make a collection of all the biggest lessons I've learned?" That would fill them. And besides, I wouldn't have to compromise on what to write about. I could write a few pages about every concept I found interesting and meaningful.

I then began to think of an audience. "Who would be interested in reading this book? And who would I personally like to share my lessons with?" The immediate answer was my brothers. If I could share my biggest life lessons with two of the people I cared most about, then I would be happy. That would be worthwhile and close to my heart.

When I got back from the walk, I immediately started writing.

Part I

Healing

Embrace the Pain

"We are healed from suffering only by experiencing it to the full."
—Marcel Proust

Growing up, I experienced my fair share of pain and suffering—just like you; and probably like any other kid on the planet. To suffer is surprisingly normal, but it's hard when you're young and you don't know what to do about it. Although some people like to think that being a child is easier than being an adult, I disagree (I couldn't even avoid peeing myself when I was laughing); it's only through living for a while—through experience and knowledge—that you learn how to deal with life and its difficulties.

One of my first knocks with genuine pain was back in elementary school. I had a crush on a girl in my class, as she was cute, kind and funny—the whole package in a 12-year old's eyes—and she even acknowledged my existence. Although I liked her, I was too shy to express it in person. And since telling her face-to-face was no option, I did the only other sensible thing I could think of and asked her to be my girlfriend through a text message.

As I anxiously waited for a reply, my heart was beating like mad. I couldn't sit still. When I finally got it, however, it might as well have stopped. My first rejection was now a fact, and the pain of heartbreak came rushing in.

This experience was painful unlike any other I had encountered. I was used to bruising my knees and not getting my will, but this was something else completely. This was suffering. And as I had no clue how deal with it, I succumbed to a sub-par solution: I cried myself to sleep—for weeks on end—until the pain seemingly went away by itself.

Later, as I moved through adolescence, I experienced a few similar instances. I liked a girl, she didn't like me back, and it messed me up because I didn't know how to deal with the pain. Every time this happened, I would fantasize about changing my ways. I didn't want to be this shy and awkward kid anymore. I wanted to fit in with the cool kids and learn how to talk with girls. But every time though, I fell short. I couldn't force myself to change. It cost too much, and I didn't have the energy to go through with it.

It was annoying to live like this—wanting to change, but unable to—but I remained the same because I was afraid. I continued to play it small, and it wasn't until I was twenty that I experienced something that would change my life for the better. Through depression and another heartbreak—a breakup this time—I finally got the drive I needed.

In contrast to my earlier experiences, this pain was so strong that I couldn't continue to live in the same ways as before. I was shivering, tears poured from my face, and it felt like my chest was about to collapse on itself. My temples were pounding with an incredible tension, and I didn't know what to do with my body. I wanted to escape it; and I was almost tempted to that day.

Luckily, however, I chose to endure. Somehow, something inside me—something amidst the pain and infinitely small—whispered I had to change. I knew I had to find a better solution than crying, and I couldn't keep acting in the ways that had got me into the pain in the first place. I embraced it; and a new chapter of my life begun.

I had discovered my first valuable lesson and I was on my way to discover more. A new way of life had ignited.

A Less Obvious Approach

Humans naturally shy away from pain; it's in our DNA. You instinctively avoid the things that hurt you, and you quickly learn what's safe and what's not. You know that a hot stove isn't the best place to rest your hands, and it's obvious to you that you should rest them somewhere else.

However, there are times when you shouldn't avoid the pain; like when you're lifting weights, studying tough concepts, or doing manual labor. Again, this is obvious; every painful repetition build muscle, and every painful minute of effort gets the job done.

What's not so obvious, however, is an encounter with emotional and psychological pain. Feelings of depression, disturbing thoughts, anxiety, etc.—are all difficult things to deal with. And while the instinct is to avoid them—in one way or the other—it's not clear that this your best option. People seem to avoid this type of pain, more than any other; and unfortunately, it's become increasingly easier to do so in the modern world. Our smartphones are always available, and instead of having to deal with the pain in the real world, we can spend all our time in a dopamine-filled digital one. We might be connected, but it's certainly not to ourselves.

This is problematic. When you actively avoid the pain, it doesn't necessarily go away. Even if it seems like a problem might dissolve over time, the bitter reality is that you leave yourself unprepared for when it comes back around.

It's only by dealing with the pain—head on—that you learn to overcome it. You need to embrace it, investigate it, and come to terms with it (which is difficult if you keep yourself distracted). Pain is not the enemy; it's your soul telling you that something is wrong.

A Fundamental Part of Reality
One of the central tenets of Buddhism are, "Life is suffering." This does not mean that *all* life is suffering, but it does mean it's a prevalent feature in it. Happiness is also a big part of our lives, but it's important to acknowledge that suffering can always come into it. It's better to be accepting of that fact, than to have an unpleasant surprise assault you.

In one moment, we might be at the top of our health, but in the next, the merciless hands of sickness might strike us. We face problems, struggle with emotions, and are affected when those around us suffer. We go from young to old—and we'll all eventually decay.

Yet, no matter how gloom it might seem, there's something within us that can tolerate all this madness. As Albert Camus, the absurdist philosopher, said, "No matter how hard the world pushes against me, within me, there's something stronger—something better, pushing right back." We're inherently stronger than whatever suffering comes our way. We're able to endure it, learn from it, and ultimately have our lives changed because of it. No matter the adversity, we have something within us that empowers us to overcome.

Known as one of the greatest political leaders of all time, Abraham Lincoln is rarely associated with the notion of crippling depression. Although he triumphed in the Civil War, and in the excruciating battles that came along with it, it was perhaps in his internal battles he struggled the most to be victorious. On multiple occasions, his depression nearly drove him to suicide.

To say that Lincoln's life was hard would be an understatement. He grew up in poverty, lost his mother when he was a child, and experienced a variety of crushing defeats in his political career. On top of it all, his depression followed him everywhere he went.

Despite all these hardships, Lincoln came to see his adversities as a benefit. It shaped his character and helped him prepare for greater things in life. He endured it all and grew stronger because of it. Perhaps it was precisely this, his personal adversities, that shaped him into the man who could lead a nation through its.

Although Lincoln's story is unique, he isn't the only one to have grown stronger from pain and suffering. Jesus died by crucifixion yet resurrected and ascended into heaven. Oprah experienced poverty, molestation, and the death of her newborn child, yet turned into one of the greatest TV-personalities in the world. Dale Carnegie endured poverty and came close to committing suicide, but still wrote a wildly successful book on self-improvement. Even though adversity feels bad in the moment, it can help us grow stronger in the long run.

The Motivation to Change

There are different degrees of pain. It can vary from slightly annoying to outright hellish; and there are different ways in which people approach these levels.

Few will change in order to get rid of a small annoyance, because the threshold of change is simply too big. It's hard, and people are generally afraid of it (I'll come back to why in Note Five). This is why people stay in a shitty job for the rest of their lives. The pain isn't bad enough—but to risk being out of work is presumed to be even more painful. They're not satisfied, but they're so afraid of the potential negative outcomes that they're not willing to risk it.

Conversely, when the pain *is* bad enough, people will do everything they can to avoid the same thing in the future. If you break your leg playing soccer, you might become cautious of potential leg-breaking situations. If you humiliate yourself in front of your crush, you might start to avoid that person all together.

We don't like pain, and we try our best to avoid it. Paradoxically, however, the best way to avoid a similar type of pain in the future, is to embrace it in the present. We need to learn from it and understand its nature. If we don't, we leave ourselves at an increased risk of a similar event in the future.

As a soccer player, you should come to terms with the injury, let it heal, and train your leg to become stronger. As a hopeless romantic, you should figure out why you made a fool of yourself and aim to do better. Avoidance won't get you anywhere except further away from the things you love. If you want to get closer, you need to embrace and deal with the pain. Although it's not an easy task, if you want to heal from it properly, you have to set up the conditions that allow it.

When Your World Shatters
Your brain is constantly trying to make sense of the world around you. It needs a certain level of understanding in order to operate. At minimum, it needs to understand the things that will ensure your survival in the current moment.

Your brain has been doing this, ever since you were born, and it continually upgrades its representation of the world based on the information you encounter. This process, however, is extremely energy consuming. You can't keep track of everything that's going on.

14

Consequently, what you understand—your worldview—is only the easiest representation of the world that's sufficient at any moment. Not surprisingly, this might cause trouble in certain situations.

When something bad happens, your brain wants to make sense of the pain-related information (as it would with any other type of information). It does this in order to prevent it from happening again. If, however, your worldview cannot account for the pain—if there's too much of a difference between your current worldview and the new information—it will break. The old shatters under the pressure of the new (think of Kuhn's paradigm shifts, if you happen know your philosophy of science). The result is suffering.

As Stephen R. Covey, the bestselling author of *The 7 Habits of Highly Effective People*, explains it, a worldview has similar functions to a map. A map represents a territory, and its symbols explain certain aspects of the real world. With an accurate map, you'll be able to find your way. But if your map cannot account for some crucial aspect of the territory, it becomes useless. The same is true for worldviews. If your worldview cannot account for something, such as pain, you'll find it hard to navigate.

Rebuilding Your World

When this happens—when your old worldview turns to dust—a new worldview must take its place. A better one must to be established; one that can account for similar events in the future.

In order to heal properly, you need to accommodate the pain-related information. This means you have to rebuild your worldview and integrate the newly encountered information. If you make no attempts at a reconstruction, however, then you'll quickly fall back into what's familiar and hold on to your outdated assumptions about the world. This is a highroad to disaster.

If a person has been in a plane crash, a therapist might discuss with the client the probabilities of such an event reoccurring. The probability is small; and the message is that it's unlikely to happen again. Unfortunately, this might encourage the client to keep their old worldview—and not integrate the newly encountered information. When people are able to maintain their worldview prior to the painful event—despite evidence on the contrary—

they are likely to develop defenses that are more rigid. This leaves them at an increased risk for future problems.

While it's true that the probability of a plane crash is small, the probability of misfortune in a person's life is *high*. An effective therapist, who instead enables the client to reshape their world-view—with the new information incorporated—is likely to facilitate growth and healthy psychological development.

The organismic valuing theory of growth through adversity (wins the prize for 'theory with the longest name') proposes that three things need to be in place to ensure the process of accommodation: competence, relatedness, and autonomy.

- Competence refers to the tools at your disposal, and the ability to deal with the pain (more on this in Note Two).
- Relatedness refers to the social environment, and the support you get from of others (more on this in Note Three).

- Autonomy refers to the freedom and the responsibility you have to act (more on this in Note Five, Six and Seven).

This is what separates people in terms of their growth; and it explains why some people fall into suffering and never get back up.

If you have all three in place, you're not only likely to get through the pain, but you're also likely to grow from it. You'll be able to learn from it, develop yourself, and find the proper answers to the existential questions that will undoubtedly enter your mind. To heal from pain is to receive an update to your system—a new level of consciousness. Carl Jung, the Swiss psychoanalyst, said, "There is no coming to consciousness without pain."

This phenomenon of growing through pain isn't only historically, religiously and psychologically true; it's biologically true as well. Under the right kind of pressure and accommodation, genetic material turns on, and you become better suited to push right back against whatever is weighing you down. The stress from adversity activates the very DNA that make you grow stronger. It's an innate ability, as growing stronger helps ensure the survival of our species. In other words, you are born to handle adversity; it lies in your code.

Deal with Your Dragons

Although it feels good to escape the pain, it's nothing but a short-term solution. In the long-term, you'll be better off by facing it immediately. Research has shown that when you choose to grow through it, the reward is greater psychological well-being, closer relationships, and greater self-acceptance. You'll be able to grow stronger, more resilient, and more appreciative of life. The old saying, "What doesn't kill you makes you stronger" is accurate. If you can embrace the pain, you can grow stronger than you ever thought was possible.

If you're constantly avoiding it, however, you can't expect to overcome it either. Distracting yourself keeps you from feeling it to its greatest extent, which might be the very thing that stops you from doing something about it. Healing takes place when you experience it to the full. As Khalil Gibran, the Lebanese American poet, said, "Your pain is the breaking of the shell that encloses your understanding. It is the bitter potion by which the physician within you heals your sick self." Mike Posner, the American singer, sang, "If you want to move on, feel the pain."

So, instead of looking at your phone, look inside and deal with your dragons. Listen to what's going on and prepare for a fight. Be patient, however, because healing is often a gradual process. But if you keep at it—with everything you got—you'll eventually learn to overcome it.

You can't control what happens to you, but you can control how you respond. No matter the intensity of the pain, you can choose to embrace it. And while it's not fun (it's pain after all), it's worth it.

Embrace the pain, and let it transform you.

Suggestions on How to Make Use of This Note

- Accept and internalize that pain can be random sometimes. Bad things can happen to good people.
- Sit down and be quiet. If you're currently struggling with something, allow the painful

feelings to come to you. Don't force it; just feel its presence upon you. Acknowledge its existence.

- Apply the accommodation-tools in lessons Two, Three, Five, Six and Seven.

Articulate Yourself

"If the tongue had not been framed for articulation, man would still be a beast in the forest."
—Ralph Waldo Emerson

I felt lost after the breakup. I was confused about how it came to be; and to make matters worse, the depression that had crept in on me before it took place was now in full blossom. The pain covered my being and filled even the tiniest cracks with ache. It lay on top of me, like a stone that wouldn't budge.

During the first few days, I struggled to keep sane in the daytime; as I imagined it was going to be like this forever. At night, I got to escape the pain, but only if I was lucky; even here, throbbing nightmares struck me on occasion.

While dreaming about the breakup was painful, the ever-present guilt that followed me in the waking hours was even worse. I didn't know why, but I felt unreasonably guilty for the way it had ended (at present I know it's a classic symptom of depression).

Borne out of this remorse, I started to construct an apology on my phone. And although it started just as that—a simple apology—it soon became a thorough explanation of what had happened; an outlet for the feelings inside. It eased my guilt. But more than that, it helped me understand.

Through writing, the confusion lessened, and I came to understand how the depression had influenced my breakup. Because although I had been feeling sad prior to the relationship, it wasn't until after I entered it that I fully realized the scope of my sadness. The contrast became clear. The newfound spark of the relationship—which I knew was supposed to feel good—was quickly replaced with hopelessness, weary and confusion. I turned deep into my own shell—cold and out of touch—and I was unable to step outside the illness. I slowly turned unfit as a partner and the breakup became inevitable.

As I wrote and reflected over these things, I felt the pain ease away. It directed my attention to something constructive, rather than self-loathing and destructive.

For several weeks, I continued to write and rewrite everything I could remember about the day of the breakup—and everything leading up to it. Every detail, the sequence of events—what she said, what I said—had to be crammed into the small amount of space that was in the notepad of my phone. I was never satisfied, however, and I repeatedly revised the apology. I wanted to make it as clear as possible, but never felt like I could truly articulate what had happened.

This whole process was addictive. Because as I increased my understanding of what had happened in one end, I could feel my pain lessen in the other. As a consequence, I became obsessed with making it perfect. I had to fill every emotion, regret, and explanation into the apology, and I didn't want to stop before the pain was gone. It was compulsion.

After several weeks of intense writing, I had by far bypassed the level of clarity I needed. I had understood everything to a sufficient degree, and I was finally able to stop. Although extreme, I had taken an effective first step in the process of healing from pain—and without even intending it. I had begun the process of accommodation; I increased my competence by increasing my psychological understanding of the situation. I had learned another lesson: I had articulated myself.

The Pen and the Sword

When she was just a young girl, Helen Keller lost her sight and hearing to a severe childhood illness. As a result, she lived in total darkness—completely isolated from the rest of the world; and struggled to orient herself as a consequence. It wasn't until her teacher, Anne Sullivan, held her hand under a stream of water—all the while spelling *w-a-t-e-r* with a manual alphabet in the other— that she finally awakened to a comprehensible world. Now, as she started to articulate, conscious thoughts emerged.

This is how she explained it herself: "I stood still, my whole attention fixed upon the motions of her fingers. Suddenly I felt a misty consciousness as of something forgotten—a thrill of returning thought; and somehow the mystery of language was revealed to me. I knew then that 'w-a-t-e-r' meant the wonderful cool something that was flowing over my hand. That living word awakened my soul, gave it light, hope, joy, set it free! ... Everything had a name, and each name gave birth to a new thought.

As we returned to the house every object which I touched seemed to quiver with life ... I learned a great many new words that day ... words that were to make the world blossom for me."

To articulate something, means to put an idea or a feeling into comprehensible words. It's a conscious apprehension of reality.

If you're clear, precise and thoughtful in your articulation, then the likelihood of a misunderstanding is almost zero. This is good—for both you and for the world—as *you* need to understand yourself; and *others* need to understand you as well. If you're properly articulated, you'll be an effective, competent individual— with plenty of opportunities in the world. People flock to good communicators; as they want to business with them, stay up late just to talk with them, and explore new concepts in their proximity.

As the pen is mightier than the sword in our modern society, proper articulation is a great power to hold. We fight our battles verbally (unless you're an eight-year-old crybaby or something), because that's the norm in a highly developed world. There's really no need for violence—only a need to articulate ourselves and listen.

Although it's hard to accomplish in practice, there's utility in truthful, honest communication: We're all responsible for making sense of the world we're living in, and we might as well make it as good as possible.

Understanding and Manipulating the World

According to an interpretation of the Bible, at the beginning of time, God spoke the world into being. Through word alone, he transformed the chaos of nonexistence, into the orderly known of existence. By articulation, he created the world. By articulation, you have the power to do the same. You're a child of God.

Whatever your relationship with religion, you do have the power to increase your conscious understanding of things, through naming and thinking about them. By thought, you can turn something fleeting into something firm, and bring new concepts into reality. Through proper articulation and precision in thought, you make sense of the world around you.

It's this ability, to think consciously, that sets us apart from the other species on earth. We are more or less capable of understanding reality—and we can even manipulate it if we please. By abstraction of though, we

27

can think of things we cannot currently see, touch or feel—and we can even play with alternate realities.

You have the power to transform the world. And it starts within your mind.

Due to these incredible powers, it matters how well we can articulate something; our comprehension of reality depends on it. Proper articulation makes things easier, and poor articulation makes things harder.

The quality of an intimate relationship, for example, depends on the communication between partners. If it's bad, the relationship falls apart due to unnecessary arguing, misunderstandings, and the lack of closeness that good communication inevitably provides. If we're unable to understand our partners—and they us—then the chances of developing a quality relationship are small. The same is true for any relationship.

It's also the case in situations where we're trying to communicate an idea—through text or speech. (I realize I've set myself under pressure).

Poor communication isn't at all desirable, and at its extreme, it can have serious consequences.

In 1914, the assassination of Archduke Franz Ferdinand of Austria took place, and it signaled the start of one of the largest wars in history.

It was June, and the Archduke and his wife were on a harmless motorcade through Bosnia. Most people welcomed their visit, but not everyone was pleased as political motives had given birth to a conflict. As a consequence, a terrorist disturbed the peace when he launched a hand grenade towards the royal couple's car. It missed, but exploded near the vehicle behind them.

Affected by this dramatic incident, the royal couple still went to their scheduled reception at Sarajevo's City Hall. But after this visit, plans were changed so that the couple could check on those injured in the attack, at the hospital.

Due to these changes, confusion spread among the drivers. In the midst of it, instructions were unclear—poorly articulated—and it caused the driver of the royal couple's car to head down the wrong avenue. The driver noticed after a while, but as the car made a turnaround in one of the side streets, a young man sitting at a café spotted them. It was a conspirator named Gavrilo Princip, part of the same terrorist organization that had struck earlier that day, and the opportunity of his lifetime was given to him. He made his way to the car, and without hesitation he killed them. The terrorists achieved what they had planned for, and soon after, hysteria unfolded over Europe. World War One had begun.

It's uncertain if it would have happened otherwise, given proper articulation of the instructions. But what is certain, is that poor articulation can lead to disaster.

Writing as Therapy

A great way to improve your articulation is by writing. In contrast to plain thinking, which is unorganized, writing is a structured approach to thought. As you probably know from experience, the mind can be a real mess sometimes—and especially if there's something intense going on. Writing, however, can bypass many of the messy storms, and allows you to create a consistent, coherent line of thought. It creates a natural space for reflection, and it allows you to gain important insights about yourself and your environment.

As you write, the mental representation of your thoughts changes. It makes them more objective. This in turn makes it easier to observe and detach from them, as you can easily see and follow your structure. When you write, problems appear more readily and faulty thinking shines through.

If, for example, you're struggling with a difficult emotion, then naming that emotion will alleviate some of its power over you. Instead of it being a fuzzy number of unknown reasons, you pinpoint it down to a limited, graspable entity. This makes it easier to handle. If you reflect on its nature as well—its origins and its impact on you—it will become even easier. The known is easier to deal with than the unknown; you have to know what your problem is before you can do something about it.

This relates to the requirement of competence, which I previously linked to the accommodation of pain. By increasing your understanding of something, you increase your competence of it as well. When you know what it is, you can figure out what to do about it and deal with it more effectively.

Past, Present, Future

You can also rewrite a pain's significance. You can turn it into something positive and make a meaningful incorporation of the pain-related information. And whether the pain was random or of your own creation, you can make it meaningful. You can make it matter in your personal story; and see it as the great obstacle that you fought and overcame. You're the one holding the pen, so you might as well make it a triumph. How you frame it matters.

By rewriting its significance in the past, you make it matter as you continue to live into the future. You turn it into personal power.

Through articulation, you can also, precisely, write out the structure of your future. You can increase your understanding of what's possible, and you can play with various paths without actually having to live them. You can set goals, make plans, and strategize. You can look into the vast unknown while sitting in the comfort of your own home. You can think ahead, achieve clarity, and increase your understanding of where you want to go in life (more on this in Note Six).

As well as the past and the future, the present is malleable too. This was portrayed in the example of the difficult emotion. You have the power to reframe the present moment, and in an instance, change your perspective on life. You can choose to see the good, be grateful for what you have, and realize that the present moment can be beautiful if you allow yourself to see it.

Articulation allows you to think of yourself, others, and the entirety of life—past, present and future—in a more sophisticated manner.

Input from Reading

Another way to improve articulation is through reading. As H. P. Lovecraft said, "*One superlatively important effect of wide reading is the enlargement of vocabulary which always accompanies it.*" When you expose yourself to a wider vocabulary, coherent linguistic structures, and quality articulations—you increase your own ability to articulate as well.

As you read, you'll also encounter novelty. New ideas, new arguments, and new ways of thinking about the world. You might even come across new words; when you do, look them up and discover their meaning (here's a new one for you, hopefully: "Pertichor.")

I was quite fond of reading when I was younger. As I grew older, however, I abandoned it completely (except for in relation to school). I figured it was a waste of time. When I was a little older than that again—when I found myself in this aftermath of the breakup—my love of reading ignited once more. I was in desperate need for information.

In companionship with all the writing I did, I also did a fair bit of reading. As I wanted to learn more about my situation, but was unable to discover everything through introspective writing, I turned to outside sources for information. Naturally, I started at the most sensible place, and asked Google what was wrong with me. And after encountering the obligatory misinformation that comes along, I finally came across more credible sources.

I started to read psychology, philosophy, and general self-improvement, and I could feel the effects it had on my psyche. Through a quest for self-knowledge, my competence raised, and I was able to deal with the pain. It was healing through text; bibliotherapy.

The Legacy from Socrates
Proper articulation isn't only beneficial to the individual, but for the whole society as well.

Through dialogue, we understand the world together. This was Socrates' great realization. We can find out what's important—truth, morals, and proper being—by exchanging our ideas and having honest discussions about them. In dialogue, our ideas battle it out—rather than our bodies—and the strongest are the ones who survive. Our ideas die instead of us; and that's how we gradually improve the world together. We get a glimpse of each other's world-views—and we find holes in our own. Together, we create a shared understanding of the world.

As Jordan Peterson, the Canadian psychologist, said, "Speech matters, because that's how you turn potential into reality." When we explore the world together—with proper articulation—we turn the unknowns into knowns and expand our conscious understanding of it. That's the purpose of language.

It also makes it clear why we shouldn't lie. Not to ourselves and not to others, because lies corrupt our shared understanding of the world. If we lived in a world of falsehood, our survival would be at risk. We wouldn't be able to distinguish right from wrong, and our whole experience would have turned into a gamble where no one ever trusted each other. And as we couldn't have been sure of anything, it would have made us weak and vulnerable. There would be no right answers to our problems. As John Snow said, "When enough people make false promises, words stop meaning anything. Then there are no more answers, only better and better lies."

Things turn bad when people lie. Just think of what would happen if you constantly lied to yourself. Fyodor Dostoyevsky explained it best: "The man who lies to himself and listens to his own lie comes to such a pass that he cannot distinguish the truth within him, or around him, and so loses all respect for himself and for others. And having no respect he ceases to love, and in order to occupy and distract himself without love he gives way to passions and coarse pleasures, and sinks to bestiality in his vices, all from continual lying to other men and to himself." Without proper, truthful articulation, man becomes a beast in the forest.

Tell the truth, because lies are eventually exposed. The truth, however, will stand the test of time.

Suggestions on How to Make Use of This Note

- Pick up a journal or create a new document. Think of something—this could be past, present, or future concerns—and just let the words flow out without thinking too much about them.

- Put a distressing feeling into words. Name it and reflect on its nature.

- Read about something of interest, or something you want to know more about. Grab a book or search the internet (beware of bad sources however).

- Have a dialogue with a friend or colleague. Be honest in your approach and be precise in your articulation.

Seek and Give Support

*"Anything is possible when you have the
right people there to support you."*
—Misty Copeland

Throughout my teenage years, I didn't really discuss my feelings with anyone. I kept quiet about the things inside; and especially when it came to the big things. Although it might have been a byproduct of boyhood, it nonetheless came to a point where it was difficult to keep it all to myself. Que the heartbreak and the depression.

Flooded with pain, I initially continued in my usual manner. Silence; I once again chose the lone knight strategy. This time around, however, it was one hell of a battle, and it quickly drained my resources. The pain consumed all of my energy, and it made it difficult for me to do other things besides focusing on the pain. I did, however, manage to write and read—the two weapons I was most comfortable to wield. And although these tools were of great benefit to me, I still felt like there was something missing in my arsenal. I needed something more: I instinctively longed for human support—and the love and empathy that came with it.

While I knew that asking for help was a smart thing to do, I couldn't force myself to do it. I was afraid—inexperienced in crossing that type of interpersonal barrier—I was stuck. What I secretly hoped for, instead of me asking, was that someone would notice how I was feeling and initiate the first step. After all, I was feeling all this pain on the inside, so how could it not appear on the outside?

I patiently waited, but no one ever made the conversation I was hoping for. And therefore, after a long period of depressive isolation, it finally came to the point where I couldn't wait anymore. I began to exaggerate my behavior, to such a degree that it was obvious that I was struggling with something. I kept my head down, slouched, and moved in an awkward, painful manner. Naturally, someone picked up on this unusual sight and asked me how I was doing. The opportunity had been given to me, and I took it; I told my mother what was going on.

This was a huge relief. My breath eased, and a tiny spark of warmth filled my body. What had gnawed on me for so long was finally out in the open. And for the first time in months, I didn't feel alone on the battlefield anymore. I had crossed the threshold into human connection, and I immediately started to heal in a better way. The fact that I told someone lifted a giant weight off my shoulders. Now, with replenished energy and a new lesson learned, I could continue to fight bolder. I had support, and it didn't take long before I was completely free of the pain.

The Courage to Ask for Help

In our darkest times, it can be hard to see past the glooming horizon; and yet alone the hands reaching down from heaven to help us. When we're in most need of support, it can feel like there's none. Our problems shadow our perceptions—that's a paradox of mental disorder.

Although we might want support more than anything, it can be far too easy to hide. That's the safe thing to do; as we don't want to appear weak, vulnerable, or as if there's something wrong with us. Limiting self-talk flash through our minds, and themes such as, "What will the other person think of me?", "Do they care?" Or "I don't want to trouble them", are common. But whatever the reason, there's no doubt that asking for help is scary.

This makes it only natural to want others to initiate the contact—to pass on the responsibility to them. But in most cases, *you* might be the one that have to do it.

While it sucks, the reality is that most people won't notice your pain. They can't read your mind and infer that something is wrong. Even though you might feel like your pain is radiating, there might be no one coming for you.

If, however, they knew exactly what was going on, the majority of people would have come your aid. But it's more complicated than that. They might be clueless of what to do, unsure about their own abilities, or perhaps they decide—out of a fear of an uncomfortable situation—that if there were *actually* something wrong with you, then you would surely come to seek out the support you need.

Sadly, there's a misfit in people's expectations in situations like these. You're both afraid, and it's understandable. Big problems are hard to talk about. And although initiating people certainly exist in the word, the reality is that not everyone has the capacity to do so.

The solution to all of this is simple, however, and it's to take the initiative yourself.

Although it's challenging, you have to find the courage to ask. You must dare to be vulnerable and expose yourself to the world. You have to override the fear of appearing weak or at fault. Because as Viktor Frankl said, "There was no need to be ashamed of tears, for tears bore witness that a man had the greatest of courage, the courage to suffer."

Although you might hesitate, know that it's extremely likely that people will help you once you offer them the chance. They don't want you suffer. They care about you. Your happiness. Besides, the person in position to help you would probably have wanted the same from you. It's each turn to be there for support, as you might each suffer at different times in your lives. To help is a human interest. If someone asks, it's an honor to be there.

If you open up to someone you trust, they will come to your aid. And if, however, you don't feel comfortable talking to anyone you know of—whatever the reason, know that there's people out there that *does* want to help you. You can always seek out a psychologist or other healthcare professionals. They will listen; they will care. They will aid you in healing yourself.

Strengthening Yourself and Others

Seeking support is one of the cleverest things you can do. The act itself is noble, character strengthening, and all in all just a wise move. It shows that you understand you can't deal with everything by yourself; it shows that you acknowledge the need for others, as you can't possibly know everything yourself. Even Socrates recognized this fact, as he said, "I am the wisest man alive, for I know one thing, and that is that I know nothing." If you look past the humblebragging, the message it holds is true: You have gaps in your knowledge. But other people might help you fill them.

In a supporting relationship, everyone grows—and not just the person in need of it the most. The old adage "Two heads are better than one" rings true, because together you can do far more than you can on your own. You can build each other up, advance together, and even exchange resources. There's also innovation, new ideas, and a plethora of new opportunities. Together you are more; cooperation benefits all. It's synergy.

Napoleon Hill, the famous author of *Think and Grow Rich*, described the phenomenon like this: "It is the principle through which you can accomplish in one year, more than you could accomplish without it in a lifetime, if you depended entirely on your own efforts for success." One plus one is more than two.

Together, you can explore and articulate problems— as well as to find their solutions. When there's more than one person seeking to understand something, a conversation can uncover Atlantis.

The power of a conversation lies in the spontaneous nature of talk, as it tends to bring spontaneous solutions. One person might say something, which stimulates the other person to think of something they haven't thought before—and vice versa. This process goes back and forth, and each are prompted into increasingly deeper territory.

When you're in a conversation, you have to make what you say understandable. You must articulate yourself in a manner that makes it possible for the other person to comprehend what you're saying. This in turn, allows you to understand yourself as well. From the moment the words leave your lips, you can hear them as if they were new. Inside your mind, your thoughts might be vague, but when you get them out in the open, they solidify. Through conversation, you bring unclear concepts into understandable words

We Exist for the Sake of Each Other

A relationship can heal the soul. This relates to the requirement of relatedness, which I mentioned back in Note One. To feel a certain kind of relatedness to other people—to feel like you belong—is an important part in dealing with pain. Because when you're cared for, and listened to, it feels good. It acknowledges you as a person. It signifies that you matter. It shows that you're not alone.

Conversely, loneliness can be damaging to your health. It scars your mental, physical and spiritual well-being; and it hurts because we evolved to be together. The reason it evolved, is because together has made us stronger. We make faster improvements this way, we can easily exchange resources, and it increases our chances of survival. Over time, this has turned us into highly social animals. As Marcus Aurelius, the Roman Emperor and Stoic said, "We exist for the sake of each other."

A Few Words on Helping

Support doesn't mean that someone can just sit back and watch other people fight their battles. This won't do any good. The way to strength is through—and people will not emerge stronger if someone else does the job for them.

People don't need "help". Not directly. They need an aid in helping themselves. It's *their* problem, and not anyone else's. They have to learn how to solve it themselves. The job of a supporter is simply to create a space in which people are able to deal with the pain themselves.

Networks of People

In his hit song, *God's Plan*, Drake rapped, "Imagine if I never met the broskies." This line is an acknowledgment. He knows that his success isn't only on him, and he values the support of his brothers.

Before he was a famous rapper, Drake lived a simple life in Toronto with his mother. Here, he had his bar Mitzvah and attended high school.

His transition into entertainment happened through a classmate whose father was an agent. His father had said something like, "If there's anyone in the class that makes you laugh, have them audition for me." The kid had immediately thought of Drake, which went on to nail the audition and got himself his first agent. And it didn't take long before Drake was able to land an acting role on a series called *Degrassi: The Next Generation*. Here, he played his role for seven years.

Acting wasn't Drake's only talent, however, and he recorded a few rap-songs in his spare time. The transition into the music-scene happened when someone picked up on one of his songs and played it to Lil Wayne—a song which featured his vocals. Now, in a stroke of luck, just as the termination of Drake's role on *Degrassi* took place, Drake received a phone call from Lil Wayne himself, who invited him to join him on his tour. Drake said yes, and that was the starting point of his music career.

If you noticed, Drake's key to advancement—in television, music, you name it—was through other people.

Few people reach success alone. And when you know the right people, you can advance a lot faster. That's why networking is such a popular concept in the world of business. It's understandable, because support is an excellent tool in problem-solving—and in business, *solving problems is what creates business.*

In networks, people tend to return favors. This relates to the principle of reciprocity, which we're evolutionary wired to uphold. Let me give you an example of how it works: If you do me a favor, then I feel compelled to return it at some point. I know that if I do, everyone will get along better, and perhaps, it's more likely that you'll do me another favor in the future. This reciprocity should ideally go back and forth, and it's why some people feel guilty when they receive a present but have not prepared anything in return.

As social animals, reciprocity keeps us interacting with each other. We have traded resources for thousands of years, and to uphold the principle of reciprocity is to uphold a sense of peace. A violation of it diminishes trust. As Seneca, the Stoic philosopher, said, "Our fellowship is very similar to an arch of stones, which would fall apart, if they did not reciprocally support each other."

Although this back and forth might not work all the time, as there's always people who knows how to exploit this social phenomenon (psychopaths being the extreme example), it's reasonable to suggest that it works for the best in the long-term. Because no matter the outcome in the short-term, giving to people will do you good in terms of a reputation. And besides, giving is a good thing in of itself.

Home

Support is like a safe haven in the darkness. From here, we can go on our own adventures, with the knowledge that we can always return back home. We can explore, we can fail—and go back to safety when we need it.

We're not born to go through existence alone; we're born for the sake of each other.

Now, although we have the power to do a lot by ourselves, getting the support of others can bring us to a whole other level. And the empathy, belongingness, and love that comes with it gives life a fair bit of meaning. Hence, we must be brave enough to seek it, and strong enough to give it. We must show our fellow beings that life is worth living together.

Suggestions on How to Make Use of This Note

- Whenever you have a problem, don't be afraid to seek out support. Try to understand it and solve it together.
- Practice vulnerability and the art of sharing what's on your mind. You can start with something small, and then build on from there.
- Think of someone you can enter a supporting relationship with. Who can you help? And who can help you?

Part II

Preparation

Observe the World

"You can only find out what you actually believe (rather than what you think you believe) by watching how you act. You simply don't know what you believe, before that. You are too complex to understand yourself."
— Jordan Peterson

I discovered the idea of self-observation in the first summer after my breakup. I was still reading a lot, and one of the articles I encountered was about mindfulness, which is the psychological process of bringing your attention to experiences in the moment. While the article had several interesting points, the idea that really made an impact was the idea of being mindful of *oneself*. It struck a chord, and I immediately wanted to try it.

At my next shift at the grocery store I was working, I began to observe myself and what I was doing. I knew from my earlier shifts that I tended to stress more than needed at times; and with this distinctive phenomenon in mind, I tried my best to identify what was causing it.

Every time I felt a wave of stress-hormones rush in, I tried to catch myself and analyze the situation. And it didn't take long before I discovered the cause of it: A lot of customers around, and not enough employees to handle it. In other words, chaos.

Now that I had learned the nature of the stress, I could deal with it more effectively. Whenever I noticed the rise of a chaotic situation, I would simply manage my response. I stopped engaging in the thoughts and feelings that accompanied the situation, and I allowed them pass by themselves. I had identified the problem, and thus, I was able to improve my satisfaction. A lesson wiser, my shifts became much less stressing.

Stories of Wisdom

On the American dollar bill, there's an eye at the top of the pyramid. It sees everything and watches the workings of the world. No, I'm not hinting at illuminati, but to something much more exciting: *the idea of observation.*

This eye of providence, or "the all-seeing eye", represents the eye of God as it watches all over humanity. And this is the interesting comparison: we equate the ability to observe with God-like powers. And we do this because if you take the highest (God-like) perspective, you'll be able to observe more than if you take the perspective of your subjective (human) experience.

You see (pun intended), over the course of evolution, humans have observed each other, and through it learned to differentiate between what works and what doesn't in the world. We have then told stories about it to secure the wisdom.

The most important stories—the ones with the most important messages—have survived from generation to generation. The stories of little importance have been lost in the river of time.

The Hero's Journey is such an example. In short, it's a pattern of confronting the unknown, finding gold, and bringing it back home—and it's found in a variety of stories.

A modern story that follows this pattern, is the story of Bilbo Baggins in *The Hobbit*: Bilbo goes on an adventure, into the unknown to face a giant dragon. And once he's out there, he encounters things of great value (a precious ring and whatnot). Finally, he returns home with stories of wisdom and a chest of gold. That's a valuable pattern worth repeating.

Science tries to do the same thing as stories. Scientists observe the phenomena occurring in the world, and subsequently tries to increase their understanding of them.

Now, if you would take a close look at yourself and those around you, then you too would be able to notice the patterns of value. You would observe that some things work better than others do, and that there's specific patterns of behavior that lead to success. If you could manage to extract their lessons—and use them—you too would be on your way to success.

Pay Attention

In order to observe yourself, you need to pay close attention to what you're doing in the present moment. This is hard, however, and especially in the digital era. With thousands of sources competing for your attention, it's incredibly easy to get distracted.

Even though it's hard, paying attention is still a worthwhile activity. Because if you're not paying attention, you might miss out on the opportunities around you—and not to mention the opportunity to know yourself.

In one of the most horrifying quotes I know, Erich Fromm, a German psychologist, exemplifies what can happen if you don't know yourself: "Today we come across an individual who behaves like an automaton, who does not know or understand himself, and the only person that he knows is the person that he is supposed to be, whose meaningless chatter has replaced communicative speech, whose synthetic grin has replaced genuine laughter, and whose sense of dull despair has taken the place of genuine pain. Two statements may be said concerning this individual. One is that he suffers from defects of spontaneity and individuality which may seem to be incurable. At the same time it may be said of him he does not differ essentially from the millions of the rest of us who walk upon this earth."

If you want to know yourself, start to observe yourself. Pay attention and increase your awareness of what makes you. It's the baseline for personal development. As

Auguste Comte said, "Know yourself to improve yourself."

Observation

If you would like to increase your self-understanding, you could start to observe yourself as if you didn't know who you were. Try to tilt your viewpoint towards objectivity and watch yourself as if you were watching a movie. Detach and watch from a meta-perspective.

This is a difficult task, however, because your immediate experience is mostly subjective. You're in it—part of your continuous being—and it's hard to get away from that fact. The subjective nature of who you are, makes it hard to get an honest and unfiltered look of yourself. You're prone to bias and self-deceit. But remember, just because it's hard doesn't mean you shouldn't try. Any increase in self-knowledge is better than turning into an "automaton."

Through self-observation, you can discover a variety of things. You can, for instance, find out what you value. Because when you truly value something, you embrace it with your very being—and your actions leave clues to just how much you value it. This is different from what you think you value, because actions are the strongest representation of who you are—of what you believe.

The structure of your values is hierarchically organized. The most important value is at the top, and the next most important below it—and so forth. From a neurological perspective, you instinctively aim for the things you value the most. As such, the top values receive more attention than the others do, because they are, after all, the most valuable. Consequently, they drive your behavior.

As an example, let's say you *think* you value productivity. To discover how much you *actually* value it, you can track how much time you're spending on it. This will expose your level of devotion.

After a few days of observation—and tracking your observations—you can reveal to yourself how productive you really are. If you discover that a host of other things takes up more time than productivity, then how much do you actually value it? If out of eighteen waking hours, only four of them was devoted to productivity, what things do you value more? There's nothing wrong with whatever you discover, but it's worth noting that it's a discovery. And that's something to improve yourself with.

You can try to observe your habits and routines, and the time spent on different activities. You might be surprised of how you're actually spending your time. For instance, how much time do you think you're spending on social media? Track it to reveal the answer (caution: it might not be pretty).

Just as your actions are observable, your thoughts and emotions are observable too. You can discover the workings of your internal world.

If you begin to practice this ability, you might draw the conclusion that you're more than just your thoughts and emotions. You're something else. While you might question this statement at first, it becomes evident when you realize that you don't act out or believe everything that goes through your mind. Just think of all the crazy things you would do if you did (you would probably lie dead under a bridge or be in jail by now). That's the case for your thoughts. But your emotions aren't any better.

They can give false representations—false alarms—of what's really going on. Think of anxiety as an example; it's a fear based on the things you *imagine* could go wrong. It's not necessarily accurate because you think or feel it so.

The conclusion is that you're simply the thing that observes (whatever that is).

Once you realize this, and practice the skill of observation, you can get through situations in a more logical and rational manner. When a thought or an emotion arises, you can question it—and analyze whether it has any importance or not. You can step back. You can call its bluff. You can recognize that your negative self-talk can be a bunch of sneaky lies.

Meditation

A great tool for learning how to observe is meditation. It doesn't require much, and you can do it whenever you like. This is an example of the process:

- Sit down comfortably and close your eyes.
- Observe your breath.
- Notice, without judgement, every time that your mind wanders away from the breath.
- Direct your attention back to your breath.

Through this practice, you can learn to notice when your thoughts and emotions enter your consciousness. And the more you practice, the better you get at watching your inner dialogue from a meta-perspective.

Tests

Social scientists have developed several tests to help you reveal things about yourself. There's many online, that's free to use, and includes tests for your personality, your strengths and weaknesses, and your social interaction patterns. They're easy to use and can give you an increased awareness of certain aspects.

Feedback

In addition to observing yourself, you can leverage the observations of others. You're inherently on tune to the social cues around you, as you need others in order to regulate your own behavior. You're not as self-aware on your own. It's mainly through others—by watching their behaviors, as well as their reactions to *your* behavior— that you get a better glimpse of who you are. As such, you need to listen to feedback and regulate accordingly.

In contrast to self-observation, where you can still choose to deceit yourself, a larger group of consensuses can tell you the truth. If enough people tell you something about you that isn't optimal—something that you weren't aware of—then it's best to become aware of that (even if it hurts your precious ego). Now, even though not every piece of feedback might be correct, it might still be helpful to consider it. Then, based on your own personal conviction, you can decide what to do with it.

In order to get a better understanding of who you are, have your friends and family give you their sincerest feedback. Have them point out your wrongs—the things you cannot see yourself. Perhaps it's worth considering your grandma's opinions after all.

Assessing Your Starting Point

Once you have a better grasp of who you are, you can start to improve more intelligently. If you want any sort of betterment, then it's a good idea to take stock of where you are. Ask yourself, "what does my current situation look like? What are my strengths and weaknesses? What is my fundamental perception of the world?" You can use the aforementioned methods to find your answers.

When you first assess your starting point and have found the areas in most need of improvement, you can start to improve your current situation. Now, it's important to fix what you already have, because there's no point in adding more stuff to your life when you already have things you can work on. That's unnecessary weight to an unstable foundation.

You first have to get the groundwork right—because everything you build on top of it is affected. Asses your starting point before you embark on your journey.

Another approach to taking stock is to switch your attention to your heroes, your ideals. Begin to consciously observe what you admire about them, and extract what you think are the best qualities in each. Then, construct an *ideal* ideal based on what you find.

If you compare that to how you're currently living, you take stock of both where you are and where you would like to go. The ideal ideal is you, because it's what you announced to be the greatest form of being based on what you value. Now the trick is getting there.

What you must remember, is to be careful not to overly rely on comparing yourself with the ideal. Because chances are, you are miles away from it. You have to keep in mind that *you* are where you are, and that *your heroes* are where they are, for totally different reasons. The key is to love yourself, but at the same time strive for more. Love your present and be hopeful about the future.

Also, an ideal isn't something you *have* to become—and besides, your ideal can change as you move through life. It's not set in stone. You might discover new things that you admire and change your course based on that. Don't worry, and don't feel bad for not being your ideal. You're young, and an ideal is simply something to aspire to.

Just try your best—to incorporate the noble qualities of your heroes. Because who knows what will happen if you try to live according to the very best you see?

Suggestion on How to Make Use of This Note

- Observe and extract the patterns around you. See if you can notice the patterns of success.
- Observe your own behavior. Watch how you react when something interrupts your daily life (e.g., stress).
- Track your time spent on different activities.

- Watch your internal states. Meditate, and see if you can notice when thoughts and feelings arise in your consciousness.
- Take tests to get a clearer picture of yourself.
- Have your friends and family give you their sincerest feedback.
- Asses your stating point. Where are you now? Where would you like to go? Look to your ideals and construct and ultimate ideal for inspiration.

Face Your Fears

"Everything you want is on the other side of fear."
—Jack Canfield

The first time I posted something real and vulnerable on Instagram, was roughly a year after the by-now infamous breakup. As I had healed and improved from the pain, I wanted to share some of the things I had learned. My life had changed for the better, and I wanted to aid people in similar situations. I wanted to inspire hope; to show that life could be better on the other side of pain.

At the same time, I also desired self-expression—to show who I had become. Because through the pain, I felt like I had transformed into someone else: a better version of myself. A tremendous change had occurred—on the inside, in my psyche—but I hadn't done a good job portraying it on the outside. I was afraid to show the new me, because the thought of breaking away from the character everyone had learned to know me as was terrifying. What if they didn't approve?

Due to these reasons, I had thought about posting something for a long time—something that was an expression of my new self. However, I was too afraid to actually do it. After all, if I posted something, then the whole world could potentially judge me (and they couldn't do that if I kept it all to myself).

This tension was uncomfortable. On one hand, I felt the desire to share, but on the other, I was too scared. Yet, I couldn't bear the tension for long, and one evening as I was preparing to go to bed, I felt an incredible sensation strike me. The desire to share had grown stronger, and it motivated me to start a caption. The words flowed onto my phone—into the same notepad I had used a year earlier to write an apology. And by the end of the rant, I had poured out my heart and constructed something that felt worthy of an actual Instagram post.

Now I was determined to share what I had written. With trembling legs of excitement, and a tightening upper of anxiety, it took me a couple of hours before I mustered the courage. But when I finally did, this is what I posted:

"Ok, so i've decited to give this a shot. Documenting and sharing my life on social media (and hopefully bring you some value). This is something that i've been thinking about for a while now, and honestly, it's scary... There are probably different kinds of subconscious fears that is present within me. Not just in this case, but in all kinds of different situations in life... I always hear that the biggest thing that is holding people back, is the fear of what other people might think. If that's the case, I will not let it hold me back. This one has actually been quite defined by me now, meaning that I can recognize it, and therefore choose to ignore it.

This kind of fear is stupid... I think we all kind of know this, but still, it's holding us back. My personal advice is this; learn abouth what fears that might be present within you. Keep a journal, write things down. Define why it's there, and think about what beating the fear can provide for you. Here is an example I wrote in my notes a while back: If the rewards of facing the fear, trumps not doing it, why shouldn't I do it? What do you think? Is there anything that's holding you back?

I'm posting this, and then i'm going to bed. I will sleep through my fears, and see how the world reacted on this when I wake up. I already have a feeling that nothing bad will happen."

As I reread this (with poor grammar and a few cringe-worthy qualities), I can almost feel the fear that was present in me at the time. The cortisol is once again flowing through my body.

Although I had worried about a negative outcome, the reality turned out to be quite different. I was right in my prediction: *nothing bad happened.* It is true what Seneca, the Stoic philosopher, said: "We suffer more often in imagination than in reality."

Now, because I faced my fear back then, I have less of a problem sharing vulnerable things today (as this entire book is an example of). I don't fear social judgement as much as I did before. I can live on my own terms, without worrying too much about what other people think of me. I'm able to show who I am; I don't fear it. I took the lesson to heart.

Action Will Redeem You

This Note is about confronting the unknown, facing your fears, and conquering the world outside your comfort zone. Dale Carnegie, the famous author and coach, said, "If you want to conquer fear, don't sit home and think about it. Go out and get busy." And that's the nature of fear: Only action will redeem you from it.

When the legendary investor Warren Buffet was in college, he specifically avoided courses that would require him to speak in front of his classmates. In the courses that he did take, simply getting up and stating his name made him terrified. This fear, the fear of public speaking, crippled him for most of his adolescence life. At the age of twenty-one, however—when he started his career as a stockbroker—he realized he couldn't continue to live in this way any longer. He knew he had to face his fears, in order to reach his highest potential. And so, he enrolled in a course on public speaking.

"You have to do it." Buffet said in a later interview. "And the sooner you do it, the better... If you have a fear of associating with people, you have to go out there and do it, and it's painful." Exemplary, Buffett faced his fear and ended up as one of the richest people alive.

The Fear of the Unknown

There's this classic story about a thief who was caught in a crime. The town's police caught him stealing a barrel of fish, and he couldn't escape when two officers surrounded him. "It's only that I'm so hungry", the criminal exclaimed. "Doesn't matter, a crime is a crime", said one of the officers, before the other said, "We'll send you to the king, and he'll decide your punishment."

When they arrived at the king's palace, the king told the man he could choose between two punishments. He could choose the rope, or take whatever was behind a big, scary iron door. Without much hesitation, the criminal decided on the rope.

As the noose slipped around his neck, the criminal turned to the king and asked, "By the way, out of curiosity, what's behind the iron door?" The king laughed and said, "You know, it's funny, I offer everyone the same choice, and nearly everyone picks the rope." "Well," said the criminal, "Tell me. What's behind the door then? I won't tell anyone," he said, and comically pointed to the

71

noose around his neck. The king paused for a while, and answered, "Freedom. But it seems that most people are so afraid of the unknown, that they immediately take the rope."

As this story exemplifies, we're all afraid of the unknown. And indeed, Dr. R. Nicholas Carleton argues that the fear of the unknown is the fundamental fear of them all. This makes sense from an evolutionary perspective: Because no one knows what exists in the unknown, we need to prepare for the fact that all kinds of threats might be lurking there. And when it comes to survival, it's better to be on the safe side—inside the realm of the known—than it's to take unnecessary risks in the unknown.

Without a doubt, fear concerns us all. It creeps up on us, distorts our minds, and stops us from achieving our dreams. Iron Maiden, the legendary heavy metal band, sums it up quite nicely: "The unknown troubles on your mind. Maybe your mind is playing tricks. You sense, and suddenly eyes fix. On dancing shadows from behind. Fear of the dark, fear of the dark. I have constant fear that something is always near. Fear of the dark, fear of the dark. I have a phobia that someone is always there."

Lessons from Psychotherapy

If there's one lesson from clinical psychology that everyone needs to know, it's this: *if you confront your fears voluntarily, one step at the time, you'll eventually learn to overcome them.* It's exposure therapy, and it works because, well, you *expose* your fears. First, you expose yourself to your fears, and then you'll eventually get to the point where you expose the fears themselves. They lose all their credibility as soon as your reveal to yourself that they're nothing to be afraid of.

This is the way it works, because your brain needs to *observe* that everything is ok. It needs to see and experience for itself that nothing bad will happen, irrespectively of what you "tell it". The part of your brain that processes fear can't understand your inner dialogue, which means that talking yourself out of fear won't help.

The only way to overcome a fear is to confront the fear and stand in it for a while—without resorting to anything to compensate for it (such as compulsively repeating calming words or pinching yourself). Your brain needs to register that everything is fine. It needs to turn the unknown into a known.

Now, if you want to get rid of a fear of public speaking (without going to a course), the way to approach it (and any other type of fear), is by making a detailed plan, involving incremental steps of increasing challenge. Here's how it might look like:

- The first step might be to speak aloud by yourself.
- The second could be speaking in front of a friend or a family member.
- Third, you could visit a stage or a podium, and stand there *without* speaking.
- Fourth, you could speak aloud, but with no attendances.
- Fifth, you could invite your friends, perhaps even some strangers—as many as you're comfortable with—and speak in front of them.
- Finally, you might be able to speak in front of a larger audience.

The success to all this, lies in pushing yourself just a tiny bit outside your comfort zone. You need to plan in such a manner that you know you can succeed in the first couple of steps. Make it ridiculously easy and move on from there.

You can also take as long as you need on each step, and you don't have to move on before you feel you can handle the one you're at. There's no need to rush. The comfort zone will gradually expand, and you'll gradually increase your confidence—as long as you keep at it.

As Eleanor Roosevelt said, "You gain strength, courage, and confidence by every experience in which you really stop to look fear in the face. You are able to say to yourself, 'I lived through this horror. I can take the next thing that comes along.'"

The Gold—and the Life Beyond

In the previous Note, we touched upon how the Hero's Journey was an observable pattern of success embedded in stories. In this one, I encourage you to be the hero in your own. As Tom Hanks, actor and filmmaker, said, "*A hero is somebody who voluntarily walks into the unknown.*"

The things you want is on the other side of fear. And the only way to get to them, is through a little bit of conquering.

Although fear might stand in the way for the things you want, you must know that it's only temporarily. There's something inside of you, just waiting to unfold; and it does once you start to expand your comfort zone. When you get bigger, the fear gets smaller. Courage is its weakness; it diminishes once you start poking.

If you can learn how to face your fears on a regular basis, then there's no limit to what you can accomplish. Success, freedom, money, love, happiness—they all await you on the other side. Just imagine. What would you do? Your best life is waiting for you on the other side.

The ability to face fear proportionally increases the ability to accomplish the stuff of legend. So go beyond what you know; make friends with the unknown. Go write your own story. Chapter 1 starts today.

Not Facing Your Fears

Marcus Aurelius said, "It's not death you should fear, but you should fear never beginning to live." We're all going to die at some point, and we might as well live the best life we're capable of in the meantime.

Although fear *can* stop us, it doesn't have to. Ask yourself, what's the worst thing that can happen if I did this? What is it that I'm so afraid of? Judgement? Failure? (Success?)

Doing something you're afraid to do isn't really the problem. You can learn to overcome them. The problem is *not* doing something you want to do. That's the difference between a good life and a bad life. Just think of how much worse it would be if you never faced your fears.

Not talking to that girl. What if she's the most capable of loving you? And you her? Would you take your chances on missing that? Would you rather play it safe, than feel slightly uncomfortable during the twenty seconds it takes to talk to her?

Not achieving your goals. What if you end up with something you hate, just because you never did what you actually wanted to do? Would you forsake your dreams out of fear? Would you really enjoy a life with the safety setting on?

Not writing that book. Would you let your innermost thoughts die with you? Would you refrain from potentially changing someone's life through your words? Would you miss out on leaving a legacy?

The truth is, we can't fulfil our lives if we're living in a state of fear. And we can't help others either. In a state of fear, we're useless. So I ask, would you miss out on living your life?

Conquer fear, and you'll have conquered the freedom to live on your terms.

Suggestions on How to Make Use of This Note

- Face your fear voluntarily.
- Break your fear into smaller pieces. Make the first step ridiculously easy to accomplish.
- Step into it and stand there for a while. Don't resort to anything to compensate for it.
- Once you're comfortable, increase the level of challenge and repeat the previous process.

Part III

Freedom

Note Six

Aim High

"Setting goals is the first step in turning the invisible into the visible."
—*Tony Robbins*

When my twin brother and I were younger, our dad made us each a longbow out of wood. They were powerful, and it amazed us how far we could make the arrows fly. At first, we simply enjoyed how far we could shoot them—a test of the bow's potential. But it didn't take long, however, before we grew tired of that simple game, and we wanted something to aim for. A tree with a smooth trunk, between the branches of another, or a big plate of Styrofoam—they were all suitable targets. Having something to aim at was a lot more fun than just shooting randomly through the air.

Professional archers have a target in mind as well: the bullseye. They align themselves with it, aim, and fire. If done perfectly, they're likely to hit center. Done well enough, they still tend to get close to it most of the time. While I'm not an expert in archery (a toxophilite according to Wikipedia), I do see a similarity between it and life in general. If everything works perfectly, you max out the score; if you face the right direction, you might still get some points for playing; and if you don't aim at all, the game becomes pointless.

Some years after the bow-shooting, I found out what it was like to play a pointless game. At least, that's what it felt like. It was before the breakup, and just slightly before I entered the first stages of my depression.

It was after high school, and I had left my hometown to attend a university. But I struggled to settle in with the changes. I had haphazardly enrolled in a course, because I didn't know what I wanted; I just thought that going to the university was "the right thing to do".

I had no career plans, and no specific interest that I pursued. I had recently left behind a ten-year long dedication to sports, and so I had no clue how to spend my time now. The days were a lot longer than before. I spent most of them lying in bed, worrying about where my life was going.

One of the things I worried about, was entering the ranks of adulthood—to settle into some job that I didn't want—to repeat the same day-to-day cycle until I died. I didn't want that. But I feared it; I was clueless of any other option.

As the months went by in this new reality of mine, the cluelessness slowly turned into meaninglessness. As I had no aims for the future—nothing to aspire to and nothing to be hopeful about—I slowly drifted into depression. I had a recipe for becoming lost, and I followed it as I had nowhere else to go.

You know the rest of the story; heartbreak, changing through pain, and discovering a series of lessons. This was one of them. I learned the importance of an aim. I have one now: To write a book about what happened; to share my lessons with those who need it and aid them in the alleviation of suffering.

Clarity and Motivation

The future is a giant unknown. It's not clear what will happen, and any predictions—especially long-term—are uncertain. You can ask your local weatherman if he agrees. There's a way, however, to make it a lesser unknown: and that's by having an aim. Because when you set a goal, you set a destination to guide you through the unknown. You stake a light in the dark, and it shows you the way. You're drawn to it, like a moth is drawn to flames.

Neurologically, it works like this: Your brain follows whatever you aim for, because aims are always towards something of value—something important. You want it.

Consequently, once you have an aim, you'll notice the things that will help you reach it. As you go about your daily life, you'll start to notice relevant information, because your brain is on the search for it. If you've ever encountered a new word, and then suddenly have started to see it and hear it everywhere, then you've experienced the same effect that an aim trigger. It fixates on what's important.

Whether or not you're aware of it, you're always aiming for something. If you don't know what it is, you might blindly follow whatever your unconscious mind desire. And as Carl Jung, the swiss psychologist said, "Until you make the unconscious conscious, it will direct your life and you will call it fate." If you want to be in control—if you want to be autonomous—you have to explicitly articulate what you're aiming for.

This feeling of autonomy is the third and final requirement in the accommodation of pain. To be able to decide your aim can have healing effects on your soul. Because when you're free to choose your path in life, you can choose to be free of the pain. It's a reverence of the self.

According to the *Goal-Setting Theory*, a *specific aim* is precisely what you need in order to be successful. Establish what your aim is, and by when it should be completed. Also, set your goal *as high as possible*. Because combined, the two components will lead to an increase in motivation. When it's clear—specific—what you're trying to accomplish, you lessen the fear of the unknown. And when you have to make an effort as well—in order to reach the heights—you consequently exhort more effort.

Meaning and Responsibility

A true goal is a goal that bears meaning. And by the laws of human nature, it cannot solely be based on selfish, individual motives. It's only when an aim is directed towards something greater than oneself that it becomes meaningful.

This is how it is, because as we evolved in societies—and developed the ability to form abstractions—we went from aiming at mammoths to aiming at concepts of good. While we made do with mammoths for a long time, as we grew together in larger societies, we needed more than tasty mammoth beef jerky. Consequently, doing good in general evolved to bring a sense of meaning. And the highest good—the pinnacle of responsibility—was that which provided *the most value to our society.*

Thus follows, the more good we do—for ourselves and those around us—the more meaning we'll experience in our lives. As Leo Tolstoy, the great Russian writer, exclaimed, "The sole meaning of life is to serve humanity."

When the psychiatrist Viktor Frankl was a captive in the Nazi concentration camps, he developed the concept of logotherapy. It focused on the notion of meaning, and it concerned itself with saving people from its opposite: meaninglessness. Although Frankl himself suffered greatly by the hands of the regime, he was able to find some meaning despite it. He found it, in part, through helping others.

He said that, "The self-transcendence of human existence . . . denotes the fact that being human always points, and is directed, to something or someone, other than oneself—be it a meaning to fulfill or another human being to encounter. The more one forgets himself—by giving himself to a cause to serve or another person to love—the more human he is and the more he actualizes himself."

He then went on to say that, "A man who becomes conscious of the responsibility he bears toward a human being who affectionately waits for him, or to an unfinished work, will never be able to throw away his life. He knows the "why" for his existence, and will be able to bear almost any "how"."

If you don't have a why—a meaningful aim to guide you—then you're essentially lost. You're at risk at drifting and might even spiral into meaninglessness. And if you don't know where you're going, don't be surprised if you end up in places that you might not want to visit. In order to be in control, you need an aim. It shields you from the inevitable tragedies of life; a meaningful path is how you continue in the face of suffering.

High Goals and Smaller Goals

As mentioned, an aim is always towards something valuable. But what exactly *is* valuable, and what is worth aiming for?

A way to go about this is to look to your ideals. After you've assessed them in Note Four, you can start aiming towards them. They inspire you, because you see *value* in their actions—a reflection of what you yourself think is valuable. They've caught your attention by being good and responsible human beings. If you extract out what you see in each, and add what's uniquely your own, you have an ultimate ideal. It's what's at the top of the mountain—something valuable—and something worth aiming for.

If you're feeling anxious about this kind of aim, you're not alone. It's a big goal, and most people would fall short in its shadow. If the gap between where you are and where you aspire to be is too big, then a goal can feel more monstrous than motivating.

There is, however, a solution, and it's to *create smaller goals along the way, and focus on what's right in front of you*. This way, you can still keep your ultimate aim, but at the same time focus on completing smaller tasks as if you're climbing a staircase.

Let's say you were to run a marathon in 6 months. It would be foolish to start without preparation—some kind of completion of smaller goals along the way. If you didn't run any distances beforehand, you would surely be anxious and stressed out on the big day. You would be unsure about your abilities, and thoughts such as, "I'm I prepared? Do I have the right shoes? Oh, god, did I remember to buy enough nipple cream?" might cross your mind as you find yourself at the starting line.

These are all serious concerns (especially the one concerning nipple-safety), and if you prepared along the way, you would be more confident in your capabilities. You might think, "I've accomplished all my goals so far, so I can accomplish this one as well—even if it's a little harder." And you might even know for sure how much nipple-ointment you need.

We can agree that it's better to prepare—to have a plan with increasing difficulties along the way. The first sub goal could be running 2 km on low speed, instead of running 42 on high intensity. The next could be five. And as the weeks went by, you could gradually increase the mileage and tempo. *Half-way*, you could even run a *half* marathon.

When you gradually increase the difficulty like this, you'll be better prepared for when the ultimate comes. You'll also be able to sustain your motivation. Instead of anxiety overwhelm, you can focus on what's right in front of you.

Focus on the process, not the outcome; aim high but focus on the day. When you take each step as they come and learn what you need before you move on (or up), you'll move faster and be more content along the way. A high goal without a plan creates confusion. A plan, on the other hand, shows you what to do. It's a map to your destination.

Driven by Reasons
So far, we've stated that an aim should be:

- Specific

- High
- Generating responsibility
- Towards something of value
- Consisting of smaller aims along the way

What these components have in common, is that they create reasons for you to start chasing your goal. Because in order to pursue an aim, you need enough of them. If you don't have a reason to do something, then self-evidently you won't do it either. You need a why.

For example, as I wrote the first draft of this book, the desire to have it completed for my brothers by Christmas Eve drove me. I wanted to give them a symbol of how much I cared about them.

As mentioned in the prologue, I tried to write something for a long time before I actually managed to. But I never had the proper reasons. Until now. *When I do it for someone I care about and I have a strict deadline, I simply have to do it.* I see no other options; the reasons compel me.

What Is Your Mountain?

Mount Everest is the highest mountain in the world. Annapurna is the one with the highest fatality rate (1 out of 3!). And *your mountain* is the one worth climbing. The key issue when it comes to choosing an aim is to get it right. You need to aim for something you want, and not something you think you want, or that other people might think you should want. You must follow your own value-hierarchy (more on this in Note Nine).

If you aim at the wrong mountain, you might still reach the top, but you won't be as happy once you get there. So, before you choose an aim, think about why you would like to reach it. Is it something you genuinely want? Are the reasons for climbing it yours? How would it feel to get there?

Silence the noise and figure it out. Don't think of other people's expectations, external pressures or shallow motivations. Think of what makes you, you; and aim accordingly.

This choice, this freedom to choose what you would like to do, is at the heart of autonomy. When you're able to pursue the things you want, and take responsibility for where you're going in life, you'll be thriving, in good health—and *in control.*

What if you can't decide?

There's a lot of things to do in life. You can produce music, develop apps, play the guitar, teach, compete in sports, play poker, or do charity work. And there's a thousand other things to do as well.

Earlier in my life, prior to writing, I had the chance to try some of these activities. However, because I constantly switched between them, and never managed to commit, I never got great at any one of them. While it might be true that I made some small feats, I never felt like I achieved mastery. I half-heartedly made my attempts and never decided to get good at something. I played my options and got average at them all.

We all know we shouldn't play our options when it comes to choosing a partner (not for long anyhow). That's not how we achieve a great, sustainable relationship. So why don't we have the same mentality when it comes to choosing a creative endeavor or career?

Well, in his book, *The paradox of choice*, Dr. Barry Schwartz explains how multiple options can lead to indecision and half-commitments. Because when there's plenty of options you're always wondering whether you made the right choice or not. This keeps you from committing, and you never go all in. Consequently, you don't get very good at things either, as you don't invest enough time to develop your skills.

To decide means to end all doubt, but deciding to decide is the hardest thing to decide on.

Luckily, there's a solution. You can conduct experiments. Instead of commit to one thing for the rest of your life (which is a misunderstanding), try to go all in on something for 3 months. Be fully committed and eliminate all other options during that time. After this period, one of two things are going to happen:

- You will either discover that you were good at the thing you chose, which will lead to an increased liking and an extended period of commitment.
- Or, you will discover that it wasn't for you, have learned a lot along the way, and are ready for a new experiment.

Although it might sound scary, it's absolutely an effective method. You might not discover the thing you've been searching for at once, but you will discover *something*.

Because ultimately, you just have to pick one. You can always adjust later (more on this in Note Eight).

Søren Kierkegaard, the Danish philosopher, said, "Life can only be understood backwards; but it must be lived forwards." And that's the beauty of an experiment. You can live forward throughout its duration, and you can extract out and understand its value by looking back. It's a mini life. Go explore it.

Suggestions on How to Make Use of This Note

- Articulate an aim. Make it high and specific, with both 'what' and 'when' components.
- Take on responsibility and make your goal meaningful. Aim for something valuable.
- Construct an aim by mixing what you see in your ideals and what's uniquely your own.
- Make a plan and have smaller sub goals along the way.
- Think of your reasons—your 'why'—for accomplishing the goal. Internalize them.
- Make sure you climb your own mountain. Silence the external noise.

- Experiment if you can't decide. Try to go all in on something for 3 months.

Align Your Actions

"Suit the action to the word, the word to the action."
— *William Shakespeare*

After healing, I continued to read, watch videos, and gather information. Mostly about psychology, philosophy and personal development. Among the multitude of ideas I encountered, one of the most interesting was that of taking action. Both philosophers and entrepreneurs advised it.

This had a great impact on me, and as I was walking one day, I suddenly felt a deep urge within me to take action. I realized that thinking only had a limited value on its own. The accumulation of information had struck me: I had to turn theory into practice and act out what I had learned over the last couple of months. From that day and onwards, I focused my efforts on action. I continued to gather information, but I also tried to apply it.

Information is not Enough

Johann Wolfgang von Goethe, the famous philosopher and writer, said, "Knowing is not enough; we must apply." Similarly, Gary Vaynerchuk, an entrepreneur known for his attitude towards action, said, "When it comes down to it, nothing trumps execution." You have to take what you gather and test it against the world. You have to act it out. Because what good is information if it doesn't *do* anything?

In a world where there's no shortage of information, what separates the successful from the less successful, is the ability to turn the potential of information into actual utilization. As Derek Sivers, an American entrepreneur, said so perfectly, "If information were the answer, we'd all be billionaires with perfect abs."

Action Isn't Easy...

Jean-Paul Sartre, the existential philosopher, said, "Commitment is an act, not a word." If you, let's say, 'committed' to something in the last Note, then you have to follow through with action in this one. You must align your actions with your aim—because that's the only way to bring it into reality. Aiming without action is like pointing the remote towards the TV, without ever turning it on. You'll just be holding the remote, and you'll miss your favorite episode of *The Cleveland Show*.

An aim without action is wishful thinking. Without action, thoughts are just air that you entertain yourself with.

But I get it, action is hard. And the thing that stops most people from acting, is arguably, worrying about what other people might think of them. They feel like it's safer to hide. Because once you act, people get to judge you—and they can't do that when you keep your dreams inside.

You shouldn't feel bad about this, however, as there's no shame in being afraid of what other people might think of you. In fact, considering other people's opinions is only natural to you; you're a social animal.

It's like this, because in ancient times, being a social outcast could mean extinction. It was hard to survive on one's own back then, and to avoid being thrown out by the bouncers of the last age, people needed to behave in proper ways. If you deviated too much from the norm, you could be excluded as you meant trouble for the established sense of peace. And as such, to consider other people's opinions was a social correction tool that allowed people to regulate their own behavior.

Over the course of evolution, this ability has stuck; and we need others to give us feedback (as I mentioned in Note Four). Luckily, however, things have changed since we first started to live in communities. We don't have to worry as much about being thrown out of a certain group anymore. Thanks to technological developments, we can easily survive on our own. And besides, we can always find another community—one that's more appreciative of us—due to the global connections we have. We should be grateful for this opportunity. It allows us to deviate in the good ways.

... But it Matters

Although your evolutionary wiring tells you to care, you shouldn't have to *worry*.

Think about it. Should you let other people dictate what you can and cannot do? Should you quit on your dreams because someone *might* think something mean about what you're doing?

I think we both know the answers to these questions. Living your best life matters more than what other people think of it. Yes, you can care what others think, but you can act in your own ways regardless. You can do what you want, and simultaneously listen to the feedback that others give.

You can live your dreams, even if it's a bit scary. You know how to handle fear (See Note Five if you're unsure). You can start to act.

As you probably don't want to end up with regret, do what you aspire to. If you choose to not act out what you believe to be good, on the other hand, you're doing the world a disservice. Refraining from action has consequences too: you delay positive impact, and that's almost as bad as actively making things worse.

William James, the 'father of American psychology', argued, "Act as if what you do makes a difference. It does." You and your actions could have an immensely positive impact on the world. Act today.

When the Wright Brothers got into aviation, they didn't let anyone, or anything stop them from taking action. Even when Otto Lilienthal, a German aviator, died in an aviation-related accident, they didn't budge. On the contrary. They had followed the developments within the flight community for some time, and when Lilienthal died, they finally decided it was time to start their own experiments.

Were they concerned about the risks? Definitely. They knew that flying was a risky business—one that could potentially end their lives. But they acted nonetheless. They had an inspiring aim to accomplish—to develop a fully functioning airplane—so they had to.

And in 1903, they succeeded. With consistent action towards their aim, on December 17, they flew the first ever powered, sustained and controlled airplane flight—for a total of 59 second. That was an extraordinary achievement at the time. But had they given up due to fear, they wouldn't have accomplished it. Without action, they wouldn't have left an imprint on the world.

Another reason why action matters so much, is that it heals. To act how you want is autonomous, which aids in the process of accommodating pain. When you're able to organize your own behavior, you can act in the ways that will make you heal.

In what follows, I'll present three specific tips on action I've learned.

Habits of Success

Will Durant, one of the greatest historians that ever lived, concluded that, "We are what we repeatedly do. Excellence, then, is not an act, but a habit." What he meant by this is that a simple one-time act isn't enough to ensure excellence. Repetition is needed.

While we can choose to do the right things occasionally, that's not good enough if we want to reach our goals completely. We have to act in accordance with our aims on a consistent basis; repeat what's successful, over and over again; ingrain it in our lives and make it automatic. We need to make it a habit.

When you create a habit, you make a behavior automatic. Brushing your teeth is a classic example of one, as you do it every day and it doesn't take much to perform it.

If you can do the same thing—and make a habit out of an action that will move you closer to your goal, then it'll be much easier for you to reach it. Because if you act in accordance with your aim on a daily basis, you're likely to eventually get there.

As I wrote this book, for example, a habit of mine was to write every morning. While I might not have written that *much* every day, I did write *every* day. Now, if I was successful in aligning my actions to my aim, then you'll be reading my book right this second. That's proof that it works; daily writing eventually adds up to a book. Long-term consistency beats short-term intensity.

When you're creating habits for yourself, you might discover that it's not so easy to create them as it's to perform them once you have them. It's challenging and it can take a lot of time to implement them—anywhere from a couple of weeks to several months.

There are, however, some ways to make it easier:

- Small changes are easier than big changes. Writing one sentence every morning is easier than writing one page, etc.
- Build off from an existing habit. For example, writing, after the habit of making a pot of coffee, is easier than doing it in a vacuum. It becomes like a

chain of good habits—and you can add as many as you can manage. Start by adding an easy habit, and then once you've learned it try to add habits that are more complex.

- Prime your mind with cues. If you lay a notebook on top of your coffeemaker, it will remind you to write in it as you must touch it in order to make that sweet cup of Joe.

- Set your habits first thing in the morning. Your brain is more plastic and open to change immediately following sleep. Your mind will be fresh, and you'll be ready for almost anything.

- The biggest tip, however, has nothing to do with the habit itself. It's about what kind of reasons you have to perform it in the first place. The stronger the reasons, the easier it will be to adhere to it. You'll do what you have to do. That's it (see Note Six for more information).

Select the Right Situations

People and places influence you—and it often happens on a subconscious level. Your surroundings can shape you without your direct awareness.

Larsen, Buss, and Wismeijer, all personality psychologists, argued that, "The real answer to understanding most life outcomes can be found in the interaction between personal characteristics and life situations: exceptional things happen when chance situations meet the prepared person."

Notice that they say, "chance situations." But what if you actively designed the situations *before* you entered into them—so that it wasn't just up to chance?

Well, you do have the power to think ahead, visualize, and plan your next moves, so you can design your situations to some degree. You can think about the effects of a situation and determine whether you want to interact with it. Although it's likely that your foresight isn't perfect, it's better to anticipate some of the effects than it is to go from situation to situation unwittingly. For as Winston Churchill said, "We shape our buildings; thereafter they shape us."

If you're serious about athletics, for example, then it's not in your best interest to be in situations that hinders your performance. The gym is better than the party; and to hang out with athletes is better than to hang out with a bunch of party lions. Similarly, if you want to do well in school, hang out with other smart and determined people.

In his book, *Willpower Doesn't Work,* Benjamin Hardy tells a story about the effects of an undesirable environment.

A friend of his, called Matt, was married and on his way to his dream job. A couple of times a week, however, Matt was also hanging out with his friend Eric. And together the two would play video games, watch movies and eat a ton of junk food. Although it seems harmless, Eric was actually quite cynical and negative towards life. And over time, this harmful attitude—towards life and other people— influenced Matt to the degree that he started to develop similar attitudes himself.

He became more pessimistic, made negative remarks about his wife, and developed a pattern of swearing, which he didn't have before. Although the change was slow, it was persistent.

As Matt continued to spend time with Eric, he became more and more alike him without him being aware of it. Over a period of five years, Matt had changed so drastically that he ruined both his lovely marriage and his promising career. He had surrounded himself with a less-than-ideal, and thus, he became lesser himself.

The same principle applies to everything. You adapt to the people and places around you, and so your best bet is to cherry-pick your options.

Even though you can try to resist, it all happens automatically because you need things outside of yourself to make judgements. You need other people in order to determine what the appropriate social behaviors are. This goes back to wanting to be a part of a community and using other people as a social correction tool.

You adapt to the norm—wherever you are—and it's hard to resist that fact. So, you can either fight it or leverage it. As Jim Rohn said, "You are the average of the five people you spend the most time with." Spend time with champions, and you're likely to become one.

A Few Words on Promises

If you promise you should do something, to yourself, then it's extremely important that you do it. Why? Because when you keep the promises you make to yourself, you build credibility, self-love and confidence. Breaking them, however, can hurt your relationship with yourself (which is the most important relationship of them all).

A while back, after years of not performing a single backflip, I went to a trampoline park and discovered that I had developed a fear of doing it again. While I was able to do it in the safety of a foam-cube pool, I struggled with fear on the trampoline. I jumped up and down, waiting to perform one, but I never mustered the courage. The moment it felt right, I tightened up and failed the attempt.

I continued this way, until there was only two minutes left of the session I had paid for. Now, however, I made a *promise* to myself. I promised myself to jump in 1...2...3, and I did; I performed my first backflip in years.

The reason I did it (besides making the money worth it), was so that I could build trust and confidence in myself. I knew the ugly consequences of not keeping my promise.

While you might think it doesn't matter much, it does. If you start to become distrusting of yourself, as a consequence of breaking your own promises, then who can you trust if you can't even trust yourself? A quality relationship depends on a respectful treatment. And as you probably wouldn't take lightly on breaking promises to others, why would you treat yourself any differently?

Suggestions on How to Make Use of This Note

- Realize that your actions matter more than what other people think of them. Overcome your worries by acting out one step at the time (refer to Note Five for more information).
- Create habits that will help you accomplish your aims. See the full list of tips above.
- Design your situations before you enter them. Think about what kinds of environments and people you would like to spend time with.
- Make and keep promises to yourself.

Allow Adjustments

"When you have found that a certain wind sends you on a wrong course, adjust your sails to the Port of Right."
—*Adapted quote from Ella Wheeler Wilcox*

Before I wrote this book, I had been interested in writing one for a long time. I never managed to pull it off, however. And although I tried, I never succeeded in its development. I would typically start to write about some interesting topic, and then proceed on it for a couple of weeks. But then I would start to question myself and worry. "Was this topic for me? Was it interesting enough? Could it actually become a solid book? Was it worth my time?"

Based on the answers I gave, I usually ended up with a switch of topic, or a complete do-over of the theme I already had. I adjusted like this quite frequently, and consequently, I never got far with my writing. At first, I felt bad for it. Because after all, it never felt like I was moving forward—like a book was too big of a project.

I embarked on topics like fear, goal setting and meaning—but I never felt the drive to complete any one of them. From one topic to another, I could never stick with one; it was frustrating.

Luckily, however, I think I was right in the use of my intuition. All this adjusting led me here: it led me to write this book—a book about all the topics I found interesting and valuable.

Had I been too strict and wouldn't have wavered from my original beginnings, I would never have written these words. Conversely, if I'm now too open to adjustments as I'm writing and editing this book, I will never finish it either. The finalization of it depends on not adjusting too much, and not too little either.

Eyes Open

Before its bankruptcy in 2010, Blockbuster was the leading movie rental store in America. That was about to change, however, when Netflix stepped up the game with digital streaming in 2007. Blockbuster failed to keep up— as they didn't really believe in online streaming at the time, and so they continued to focus on their physical stores. When Blockbuster discovered the true opportunities of the online space, however, and tried to go digital a year later, it was too late. They failed to make a successful transition, and bankruptcy was inevitable. An empire faded.

In the movie rental business, one year of not adjusting was too long. How long is too long in your life?

To adjust means to change something. And it could be an aim or an approach. When you feel like something is off— when your intuition screams for a different direction— then take it upon yourself to adjust. As you don't want to continue down a wrong path for years, it's not a bad idea to turn sideways or back, when you feel like it's the right thing to do. Keep your eyes open and adjust when the moment is right.

You see, if you allow yourself adjustments, then you allow yourself some freedom. You can make mistakes, make new discoveries, and correct your course without making yourself feel too bad about it. You don't have to adhere to your original plan at all cost. You can calibrate your flight; and you can afford it. *Life is long, and it's better to arrive at the right destination than at the wrong one.* Have faith, and you'll eventually end up where you need to be. In time, you'll discover your true destination—the ultimate aim, and the perfect way to approach it.

If you don't allow them, however, you keep yourself blind. Out of ego, fear, spite, ignorance—you continue down the wrong path for years, and you might eventually end up somewhere undesirable. You'll miss opportunities, life-changing makeovers, and stagnate in your personal growth. It's self-deceit.

As such, it might not be a bad idea to be humble in your journey. You don't know everything before you start, and therefore, your initial aim or approach might be wrong. Allow adjustments.

Adjusting the Right Thing

When you feel like it's time for an adjustment, you need to consider whether it's your aim or your approach that is off.

If you truly believe in your aim—but you're moving in other directions than towards it—then you have to adjust the action-steps it takes to get there. While your goal might be fine, the approach might be wrong. You might have a bad plan, a bad method, or you might simply be afraid of going all in. So, if you've thoroughly considered and developed your goal—and you're determined to see it through—then adjust your actions. Because when you truly believe in the thing you're aspiring to, then you have to get it. If the goal is right, sail to it—no matter the adjustments or amount of time it takes to get there.

Conversely, it might be your aim that is wrong. If you're not motivated, feel genuinely dissatisfied, or can just sense that something is off—feel free to abandon the goal. Set a new one. Deep down, you know what's right, but there might be things that constrain you. You might be pleasing your ego, out of a fear of being wrong. Or you might be pleasing someone else, because you want others to perceive you in a certain way. You might even stick to a goal—and have chosen it in the first place—because you value someone else's version of success more than your own (more on this in Note Nine).

Before you go about adjusting, however, there's a caution: *Whatever you do, don't confuse hardships with the need to adjust.* Don't give up too easily the moment it gets rough. Sometimes, you have to push through. Although it might be tempting to change things and make it easier for yourself, stick with it for a little longer. Then decide what to do. Adjusting takes a certain amount of wisdom.

In Note Six, I recommended experiments as a way to test what you would like to do. The same process applies here: You can stick to something for a while and adjust when the experiment is completed. Based on what you learn, you easily stake out a new course or change the approach as you continue.

Adjusting Your Worldview

In addition to aims or actions, there's something quite different you can adjust as well. Something deeper: *your fundamental way of seeing the world.*

Although we touched upon it in Note One, I think it deserves some extra attention—and from a different perspective than pain.

In Hinduism, there's a concept called *Maya*, which explains that the external world as we perceive it is an illusion. Our consciousness plays tricks on us, and we cannot go beyond our ignorant view of the world. While we might think what we see is real, our senses are limited and they deceit us. What we really see are just fragments of low resolution; our brain fills out the rest.

Now, if things aren't working out, it might be that your way of interpreting the world isn't as beneficial as it could be. Think about it. If you aim and act on the basis of a distorted worldview, your movement forward will be distorted too. You need to adjust the premise of which you build everything else on top of.

Denis Diderot, philosopher and co-founder of one of the first modern encyclopedias, said, "There are things I can't force. I must adjust. There are times when the greatest change needed is a change of my viewpoint." Similarly, Marcel Proust said ever so poetically, "The real voyage of discovery consists not in seeking new lands but seeing with new eyes."

Now the question is; how do you adjust your worldview? Besides suffering and pain, there are other things too, that are, well, less painful. And we've already touched upon them:

- From Note Two, reading, writing and dialogue.

- From Note Three, support.
- From Note Four, observation.
- From Note Five, facing your fears and going beyond your comfort zone.
- From Note Six and Seven, having the autonomy to interact with and explore new things in the world.

When you choose to engage in these activities, you open up to a larger world of knowledge. New stimuli influence your current worldview and changes it— bit by bit—as you encounter more and more information. In contrast to suffering, where the change is more abrupt, it's not as noticeable that you're changing this way. But you do. It's a continuous process—and if you allow it, it can last through your entire life.

When something touches you, then, allow it to alter the structure of your worldview. Through new ideas, new concepts, and new understandings of the world, you'll eventually build a different, yet more sophisticated version of it.

A better worldview sets the stage for a better everything. And the more information you gather, the stronger the foundation on which you have to aim and act from. Once you improve on the most fundamental level, you improve on all the others as well.

Allow new chapters to unfold. Polish your lenses and set the premise for a better world.

Suggestions on How to Make Use of This Note

- Keep your eyes open and allow yourself to adjust. Realize you might need it sometimes.
- When you feel like you need it, consider what to adjust. Think it through. Perhaps you don't need to adjust at all—maybe it's just a little rough at the moment.
- Conduct an experiment and evaluate if you need to adjust after its completion.
- Adjust your worldview, bit by bit, by being open to it. Do it through the aforementioned activities.

Part IV

Balance

Balance Your Life

"Happiness is not a matter of intensity, but of balance and order and rhythm and harmony. Music is pleasing; not only because of the sound, but also because of the silence that is in it."
- Thomas Merton

I used to compete when I was younger. It was mostly in the sport of orienteering, and I spent a large portion of my teenage years on it. I was serious, and I wanted to perform at the highest level, and therefore I put all my eggs in one basket. There was minimum drinking, going out with friends, or staying up late. I largely avoided anything that could hinder my performance.

At present, I don't compete anymore. I work out and make sure to keep myself active, but now it's a *part* of my lifestyle, not *the* lifestyle. This all-consuming approach I used to have—with a lack of other things—was precisely one of the reasons I quit. I grew tired of the same routine; of working out, eating, sleeping. I needed more variety. And as I felt like I had missed out during my adolescence, I decided to try a "normal" life.

This transition, however, was harder than expected. I went from all sports, to almost none, and that wasn't easy on my psyche. While it was fine in the beginning, I started to feel uneasy after a while. I had left a big part of my life behind, and I experienced a sense of loss; a hole in my identity. After all, I didn't know much else growing up, and I didn't know what to do as a replacement for it.

Around the same time, I had recently started at the university. And as I mentioned in Note Six, this was when I fell into meaninglessness and depression. Quitting what I knew contributed. I traded a life *out* of balance, for a life with *no* balance. It turned out to be worse.

As you know, however, I managed to get a grip on my life again. After the heartbreak and the pain, I started to incorporate the things I wanted in my life. I shifted my balance from one-sided, to no-sided, to even-sided. I have balance now; I'm living aligned.

What's Your Balance?

The sum of your life is always in balance. It doesn't matter what you do, as long as it works for you. A life out of balance, then, means you're doing something you don't want to. That's the definition I choose to use.

If you spend all your time on one thing, that's ok. But then other things will naturally have to fall. If, on the other hand, you differentiate your life between a variety of things, that's ok too. Then you'll be more even weighted. Either way, you only have the same amount of time; there's an equilibrium.

In my case, the athletic focus once suited me, and I lived my life accordingly. When I got older, however, I felt my life tilt too much in one direction, and so I decided to switch it up.

Remember that, whatever you choose, the right balance *is the balance that's right for you.* It's your life, and so you should spend it on the things you desire—the things you most value. And even if others might perceive it as out of balance, they don't know. They can't know. You're you. And as long as you've consciously decided on how to live, you're on the right path.

Work- "Everything Else" Balance

One of the biggest challenges of balance, is supposedly that of work-life balance. In my opinion, however, the phrase 'work-life' seems to denote that work and life are separate entities. But that's not true. Work is a part of life. And we spend a tremendous amount of time on it.

Where the phrase has its origins, I don't know. But perhaps it goes back to people who once felt the need to separate the two. If work was really so bad that they didn't even want to acknowledge it as a part of their lives, I feel sad on their behalf.

What the phrase means, however, isn't really the point. The point is: life is a matter of balancing different activities, and it's your job to prioritize them. While work is (usually) a big part of life, other things such as family, friends and hobbies, are big parts of life as well (if you want them to be). It's your life and you decide. You can spend your time on sports, weightlifting, music, books, family, friends, work, traveling, etc. *But you can't do all at once.* You have to prioritize.

From a place of Value and Purpose

Whether balance is a challenge or not comes down to your approach. It's a matter of priorities—and not feeling guilty about the choices you make. If you want to spend all your time working, please do. If you want to work less and spend more time with your family, please do that instead. There are no wrong answers; it's up to you. But no matter what you choose, live according to the things you value; the things you deem as important.

In his incredibly successful book, *The 7 Habits of Highly Effective People*, Stephen Covey argues for a purpose- and value based approach to living. He proposes a 'fourth generation of time management' and goes on to explain that "It encourages you...to understand and center your life on principles, to give clear expression to the purposes and values you want to direct your daily decisions."

To determine your balance, here are some suggestions:

- Take the time to consider what's important to you. Identify your principles and values. This isn't done overnight, however, and it requires a bit of introspection.

- Based on your principles and values, consider a mission or purpose in your life. Is there a way of being that inspires you? What do you want to accomplish? How can you make a contribution to the world? How would you like to be remembered?
- Make a list of the various roles you have. What do you do on a regular basis? What are your responsibilities?
- Set one long-term goal for each role. Make it specific and time-bound, and make sure you keep your purpose in mind.
- Every Sunday (or whatever day you choose), plan your activities for the week ahead, and set aside time to work on each of your goals.

The common thread here, is that you start with your principles and values, and work your way down to the daily balance of things. When you organize your life around purpose, principles, and deep-seated values, you'll feel energized. You'll feel driven—even in times of hardship—because you'll be living in line with the proper reasons why; you'll be spending your time on what's truly important.

This way, you'll be able to live on your own terms. And while your parents, friends, and the larger society, all have opinions about what constitutes the good life, you now have a way to determine what it really constitutes. The good life is the one you've consciously decided on.

There's this story that captures a similar point, about an American executive on holiday in Southern Mexico. As he was relaxing on the beach one day, a fisherman came into the shore on his boat. The American complimented his catch and asked the fisherman how long it took him.

"Not long" replied the fisherman.

"Then why didn't you stay out longer?" asked the executive eagerly, as he clearly saw there was more room on the boat.

"Because this is enough for me and my family."

The American looked at him for a while, and then asked, "So, what do you do with the rest of your time?"

"I sleep late, play with my children and spend time with my wife. In the evening, I go into the village to visit my friends. I have a few drinks and I play the guitar. I have a full life."

The American was surprised, but continued, "I have an MBA and I can help you. You should spend more time on fishing, sell the extra fish, make more money and buy a bigger boat."

The fisherman was calm, and asked, "what happens after that?"

"Well, with the extra money from a bigger boat, you can buy more boats. And as you continue to make more money, you can eventually hire more people, buy a distribution factory, and expand your business to go international."

"How long would that take?" asked the fisherman. "Probably somewhere around ten to fifteen years" said the executive, obviously exited.

"And after that?"

"Well", said the American, before he continued, "That's when the fun starts. When the business gets really big, you can sell your stocks in the company and make millions!"

"Wow, millions... and what happens after that?"

"After that you'll be able to retire, move to the coast and sleep in—every day! You could do some fishing, play with your grandkids, and spend quality time with your wife. In the evenings you'll be able to meet up with your friends for a couple of drinks."

The executive was so excited that he was almost out of breath. The fisherman, however, didn't say anything. He just shrugged his shoulders and walked away.

There's a powerful lesson here, and it's that you shouldn't chase a false dream. Don't tilt at the windmills—as they say in Don Quixote. Don't strive for someone else's version of the good life. Live your own.

Order and Chaos

Jordan Peterson advocates a psychological reality of order and chaos. Order is the known. Chaos is the unknown. And in the balance between them, life gets interesting. It's where you should strive to be.

As you go about your life, your brain is always trying to make sense of the world around it. It needs a certain level of understanding in order to operate. At a minimum, it needs to understand the things that will ensure your survival in the current moment. This is the aspect of order — the known. Your brain craves it because its safe and predictable. You're in control here.

On the other hand, your brain craves some sort of chaos too — the unknown. It wants it because it's novel and interesting. In the unknown, there's potential; and improvement relies on a confrontation with the unknown, because it's here that new tools, new ideas, and new people can be discovered.

This interplay between order and chaos is always present in music. It's the reason why we like it so much. A quality song consists of both. It has elements that will be repeated throughout most of the song, such as a hook or a memorable melody. This is order. It also has elements that will only appear once or twice, such as different breakdowns or a bridge. This is chaos.

If a song is too repetitive, it will quickly become boring. If it has too much variety, it will be hard to follow along. A good song consists of both; it needs balance—and so does the human brain.

Flow

If you can find the balance between order and chaos, you'll enter into a powerful state of development. You'll enter flow, which is the psychological phenomenon that occurs when your level of ability closely matches the level of challenge at hand. It occurs when what you don't know, challenges what you know. It's as if you have one foot inside order, and one foot reaching out to explore the unknown. It's like tipping your toes into the water to check its temperature.

Flow feels good. It's a state of happiness. It's extremely enjoyable—meaningful—and you're deeply immersed in whatever you're doing. It can feel like time warps around you; it might actually feel like you're flowing.

The balance between challenge and competence is the foundation of flow. Mihaly Csikszentmihalyi, one of the driving figures behind the concept of flow, said, "If you do anything well, it becomes enjoyable. To keep enjoying something, you need to increase its complexity."

On one hand, when a challenge is bigger than your skill level, you become anxious and stressed out. On the other, when your skill level exceeds the size of the challenge, you become bored and distracted. Since flow is in the middle, the key to keep flowing is balance.

Mihaly (I don't want to bother you with his last name again, although, I read somewhere that his full name is pronounced like 'me high, cheeks send me high') also said that, "The best moments in our lives are not the passive, receptive, relaxing times... The best moments usually occur if a person's body or mind is stretched to its limits in a voluntary effort to accomplish something difficult and worthwhile."

When you're on the border of order and chaos, life becomes enjoyable and filled with meaning. You stretch yourself towards a better life, but you do so at your own pace. You balance the abilities you have with the challenges you aspire to. You do you.

Suggestions on How to Make Use of This Note:

- Find your balance. Prioritize between the activities you want to have in your life.
- Determine your principles and values.
- Start to consider a mission or a purpose in your life.
- Make a list of the various roles you have and set one long-term goal for each role.

- Start planning your activities on a weekly basis.
- Seek order and chaos. Seek balance and flow. Balance your level of skills with the level of challenge.

Outro

Embrace the pain. Articulate yourself. Seek and give support. Observe the world. Face your fears. Aim high. Align your actions. Allow adjustments. Balance your life.

There you have it. Nine Notes. My answer to the question at the onset of this journey. While I found it worthwhile to write this book, I hope you enjoyed reading it too. I hope you extracted some value from it, and that you'll be able to make use of some of the lessons. If, however, it did nothing more than make you think of your own lessons, then that's wonderful too.

You have valuable things to learn. I wish you the best in your discovery.

Acknowledgements

I want to thank you for reading all the way through. It means a lot.

I want to thank Marius and Vegard. I couldn't have written this book without you in my mind.

I want to thank Marthe, for supporting my writing and helping me with the editing.

I want to thank Hågen, who helped me with some of the editing.

I also want to thank every person that have encouraged my writing in general. It feels nice to have your support.

I want to thank every person online, that have brought me value ever since I was feeling lost. A special thanks goes to every contributor of Psychologytoday.com, which was the first resource that literally gave me life-changing insights.

I also want to thank Charlie Houpert, Gary Vaynerchuk, Jordan Peterson, and Benjamin P. Hardy. You have all been of great inspiration and help.

Finally, I want to thank those who discover.

Connect with Me

E-mail: jonasressem@msn.com

Facebook: facebook.com/jonasressem

Instagram: instagram.com/jonasressem

Medium: medium.com/@jonasressem

Website: jonasressem.com

Selected Bibliography

Bargh, J. A., & Morsella, E. (2008). The Unconscious Mind. *Perspectives on psychological science : a journal of the Association for Psychological Science, 3*(1), 73-79.

Barlow, D. H. (2000). Unraveling the mysteries of anxiety and its disorders from the perspective of emotion theory. *American Psychologist*(55), 1247–1263.

Biography.com. (2014, April 2). Drake Biography. Retrieved from https://www.biography.com/people/drake-596834

Britannica, E. (n.a.). Maya. *Encyclopaedia Britannica.* Retrieved from https://www.britannica.com/topic/maya-Indian-philosophy

Carleton, R. N. (2016a). Fear of the unknown: One fear to rule them all? *Journal of Anxiety Disorders, 41*, 5-21. doi:https://doi.org/10.1016/j.janxdis.2016.03.011

Carleton, R. N. (2016b). Into the unknown: A review and synthesis of contemporary models involving uncertainty. *Journal of Anxiety Disorders, 39*, 30-43. doi:https://doi.org/10.1016/j.janxdis.2016.02.007

Carnegie, D. (1981). *How to Win Friends and Influence People*. New York: Gallery Books.

Chibana, N. (n.a.). Amazing Leaders Who Once Had Stage Fright — And How They Overcame It. Retrieved from https://visme.co/blog/amazing-leaders-who-once-had-crippling-stage-fright-and-how-they-overcame-it/

Clear, J. (n.a.). How to Build a New Habit: This is Your Strategy Guide. Retrieved from https://jamesclear.com/habit-guide

Coady, S. (2017, Mars 16). Jordan Peterson on Music. Retrieved from https://www.youtube.com/watch?v=HkYa0UYStio

Covey, S. R. (2013). *The 7 Habits of Highly Effective People*. New York: Simon & Schuster.

Csikszentmihalyi, M. (2008). *Flow: The Psychology of Optimal Experience.* New York: Harper Perennial Modern Classics.

Dybvig, D. D., & Dybvig, M. (2003). *Det tenkende mennesket.* Bergen: Fagbokforlaget.

Eccles, J. S., & Wigfield, A. (2002). Motivational Beliefs, Values, and Goals. *Annual Review of Psychology, 53*(1), 109-132. doi:10.1146/annurev.psych.53.100901.135153

Festinger, L. (1954). A Theory of Social Comparison Processes. *Human Relations, 7*(2), 117-140. doi:10.1177/001872675400700202

Frankl, V. E. (2006). *Man's search for meaning.* Boston, MA: Beacon Press.

Greenspan, J. (2014, June 26). The Assassination of Archduke Franz Ferdinand, 100 Years Ago. Retrieved from https://www.history.com/news/the-assassination-of-archduke-franz-ferdinand-100-years-ago

Hardy, B. P. (2018). *Willpower Doesn't Work.* New York: Hachette.

Hefferon, K., Grealy, M., & Mutrie, N. (2009). Post-traumatic growth and life threatening physical illness: A systematic review of the qualitative literature. *British Journal of Health Psychology*, *14*(2), 343-378. doi:doi:10.1348/135910708X332936

Hill, N. (1937). *Think and Grow Rich*. Shippensburg: Sound Wisdom.

History.com. (2009, November 6). Wright Brothers. Retrieved from https://www.history.com/topics/inventions/wright-brothers

Hjemdal, O., & Kennair, L. E. O. (2014). Kognitiv atferdsterapi. In R. Hagen (Ed.), *Psykoterapi* (pp. 145-160). Oslo: Gyldendal.

Holiday, R. (2014). *The Obstacle is the Way*. New York: Portfolio.

Joseph, S., & Linley, P. A. (2005). Positive Adjustment to Threatening Events: An Organismic Valuing Theory of Growth Through Adversity. *Review of General Psychology*, *9*(3), 262-280. doi:10.1037/1089-2680.9.3.262

Kennair, L. E. O., & Kleppestø, T. H. (2016). Hva er psykopatalogi? In L. E. O. Kennair (Ed.), *Psykiske Lidelser* (pp. 13-38). Oslo: Gyldendal.

Larsen, R., Buss, D., & Wismeijer, A. (2013). *Personality Psychology*. Berkshire: McGraw-Hill Education.

Latham, G. P. (2016). Goal-Setting Theory: Causal Relationships, Mediators, and Moderators. In: Oxford University Press.

MacLeod, A. K., Tata, P., Kentish, J., & Jacobsen, H. (1997). Retrospective and Prospective Cognitions in Anxiety and Depression. *Cognition and Emotion, 11*(4), 467-479. doi:10.1080/026999397379881

Marlatt, G. A., & Kristeller, J. L. (1999). Mindfulness and meditation. In *Integrating spirituality into treatment: Resources for practitioners.* (pp. 67-84). Washington, DC, US: American Psychological Association.

Nordahl, H. M. (2014). Metakognitiv Terapi. In R. Hagen (Ed.), *Psykoterapi* (pp. 199-213). Oslo: Gyldendal.

Peterson, J. B. (2018). *12 Rules for Life*. Toronto: Random House.

Rong, N. (1995, June 19). Common Buddhist
    Misunderstandings. Retrieved from
    http://www.buddhanet.net/cbp1_f6.htm

Ryan, R. M., Aarts, H., & Custers, R. (2012).
    Unconscious Goal Pursuit: Nonconscious Goal
    Regulation and Motivation. In: Oxford
    University Press.

Schwartz, B. (2016). *The Paradox of Choice.* New York:
    EccoPress.

Segrin, C., & Domschke, T. (2011). Social Support,
    Loneliness, Recuperative Processes, and Their
    Direct and Indirect Effects on Health. *Health
    Communication, 26*(3), 221-232.
    doi:10.1080/10410236.2010.546771

Shenk, J. W. (2005, October 1). Lincoln's Great
    Depression. Retrieved from
    https://www.theatlantic.com/magazine/archive/2
    005/10/lincolns-great-depression/304247/

Sternberg, R. J., & Sternberg, K. (2015). *Cognetive
    Psychology* (7th ed.). Boston: Cengage Learning.

Sutton, R., & Douglas, K. (2013). *Social Psychology.*
    London: Palgrave.

Wikipedia. (n.a.-a). Annapurna Massif. Retrieved from
        https://en.wikipedia.org/wiki/Annapurna_Massif

Wikipedia. (n.a.-b). Blockbuster LLC. Retrieved from
        https://en.wikipedia.org/wiki/Blockbuster_LLC

Wikipedia. (n.a.-c). Hero's journey. Retrieved from
        https://en.wikipedia.org/wiki/Hero%27s_journey

Wikipedia. (n.a.-d). Oprah Winfrey. Retrieved from
        https://en.wikipedia.org/wiki/Oprah_Winfrey

Wright, J. (2002). Online counselling: Learning from
        writing therapy. *British Journal of Guidance &
        Counselling, 30*(3), 285-298.
        doi:10.1080/030698802100002326

Yalom, I. D. (1995). *The theory and practice of group
        psychotherapy, 4th ed.* New York, NY, US: Basic
        Books.